ETHICS & COMPLIANCE FOR HUMANS

Adam Balfour

Ethics and Compliance for Humans: Building the E&C Program Your Employees Deserve

Published by CCI Press, an imprint of CCI Media Group, Fort Worth, Texas

ISBN: 978-1-7350285-7-6

Editor: Emily Ellis

Designer: Gina McEuen

Author photo: Daniel Williams

www.corporatecomplianceinsights.com

CONTENTS

ETHICS & COMPLIANCE FOR HUMANS

FOREWORD

First, a confession: For most of my career, I didn't like compliance as a discipline. It was ritualistic, wooden. A formality. It seemed forced. It lacked heart.

You know what I'm talking about. Your company gets their law firm to print out a standard code of ethics, or maybe your lawyer literally copies someone else's code of ethics from the internet without permission (the irony), then changes the company name at the top. They then email it to everyone in the company and require them to "certify" that they've read it. Two weeks later, after a lot of prodding and threatening, certification is at 100%. Glad that's done. Of course, most employees never read it; they just checked the box like they're signing up for a new social media site. Those who did read it chuckled at the opening in which the CEO (in a moving opening paragraph written by PR) says, "integrity is at the heart of everything we do." Is it really?

Then there's the compliance video. The one that some compliance company sold your HR team. The 90-minute one with all the laws and legislative history and even quizzes every few minutes so you can't go off and eat lunch while it's running. Certification on that one is 100% as well. And you've got a hotline too, which you pay some other company to run for you. Don't think anyone's ever actually used it, which must mean all is well. (Or that no one can find it, since it's buried four links deep in the corporate intranet.) Put up a few compliance posters and nominate yourself for one of the 5,000 most ethical companies in the world.

Ethics and compliance programs like these not only feel insincere, they don't work. What do all the major ethical scandals of the last 25 years have in common? They all happened at companies that had a nice code of ethics and compliance posters on the wall. Hardly surprising when compliance felt like a burden, a chore.

We're at the dawn of a new era of compliance. Where leaders actually talk about acting with integrity, then walk the talk. Employees are sincerely encouraged to speak up and rewarded when they ask good ethical questions or raise valid concerns. This type of compliance uses short, interesting videos and real-life stories. It uses humor, it plays game shows. It engages people from across the company, not just HR and legal. It makes you feel proud to be part of it. It feels . . . human. And it can change the culture of a company. Adam is a thought leader in this new era.

Trouble is expensive. I'm not talking just about the fines or the class action lawsuits, I'm talking about your brand and what your employees feel every day when they come to work at a place that's not aligned with their values. Want to build a great company that gets terrific financial results? Read this book. Then sit down and think about the soul of your company and what it means to do business with integrity. More and more, the world is watching.

Robert Chesnut
Former General Counsel and Chief Ethics Officer at Airbnb and Author of
Intentional Integrity: How Smart Companies Can Lead an Ethical Revolution
(St. Martin's Press, 2020)

ADAM BALFOUR

ACKNOWLEDGMENTS

Writing a book has been a long-time personal goal of mine. I knew it would not be a solo effort, but I did not understand or appreciate how many people would play an important and valuable role in a project like this until now. Countless people have helped and supported me along the way, from giving me opportunities and helping me learn about ethics and compliance to answering my many questions, challenging my ideas and thinking, collaborating with me on new ideas and presentations, and keeping me motivated throughout the process. While it is my name that appears on the book cover, there are many people—more than I can name here—who have played a meaningful role in getting this book published and who deserve my deepest thanks and appreciation. I hope to be able to pay back and pay forward your generosity and kindness. I value and appreciate each of you and what you have done to support me.

To start, I am grateful to my colleagues. Ethics and compliance is ultimately about people, and I am fortunate to have worked with so many great professionals over the years. A special thank you to my many mentors and managers who have provided me with opportunities, as well as to the legal, compliance, global, risk, and privacy teams I have had the distinct privilege of being part of and leading. Those teams have taught me far more than I could ever hope to teach them, and I owe any success I have enjoyed to their work, effort, dedication, and care.

While I had no long-term ambitions to work in ethics and compliance, I have now realized that this profession is an unbelievably warm and welcoming community. From the many friends and mentors I have made through SCCE, Ethisphere, Compliance Week, and elsewhere, I am genuinely honored to be among this amazing group. Each of you has a challenging role, and you do this work because of your integrity and your care for other people.

Sarah, Emily, Gina, and the rest of the team at CCI, I cannot thank you enough for all that you have done to bring this book together. You have provided great guidance, helped significantly improve the draft, and put together a complete book that I am so honored to be associated with. Thank you for your patience, support, and belief in bringing this book to life.

I could not have written this book without the constant support, patience, love, and encouragement of my wife, Michelle. You amaze me every day in how you balance a challenging full-time job, doing much more than your fair share of parenting our kids and coordinating their ridiculous schedules (and much more for our wonderful family), and maintaining your sanity while I am busy working, traveling, writing, or doing my own thing. Our kids are proud to call you their Mama, and I am proud to call you my wife. We love you for all that you do and who you are to us. Thank you for reading (and re-reading) the book in draft form and encouraging me to pursue this project.

Stella, Felix, Lachlan, and Remi Jane, you are the best children your Mama and I could hope to have. Your playfulness, care and compassion for others, and your unique personalities bring us so much more joy and happiness than we could have ever imagined. Remember to smell the flowers and blow out the candles. Know that success is 10% talent and 90% effort, that you need to keep trying and keep learning, and that we love you and are proud of you each and every day. And Stella, Fefe, Lala, and RJ? Bam!

While there are many people who have been so supportive and key to this book, any and all errors contained in this book are solely my responsibility. The views and opinions expressed in this book are my personal views and opinions and do not necessarily reflect the views or opinions of any organization I have worked for or any of their employees.

ADAM BALFOUR

INTRODUCTION

WHAT DOES IT MEAN TO BE HUMAN?

Nashville, Tennessee is a wonderful city that my family and I are fortunate to have made our home. Known as Music City for the quantity and quality of musicians and importance to country (and other types of) music, Nashville has Southern charm, lots to do, and traffic that (while getting worse) is mild compared to many other big cities. It is a city that has felt relatively safe—a nice place to raise a family.

March 27, 2023 is a date that will go down in Nashville's history as a truly terrible and awful day for what happened at the Covenant School. Three nine-year old children, Evelyn Dieckhaus, Hallie Scruggs, and William Kinney, and three school employees, Katherine Koonce, Mike Hill, and Cynthia Peak, were all intentionally killed by a heavily armed individual. The speed of the police response and the disregard that the police officers showed for their own personal safety likely prevented the number of innocent lives lost from being higher than six. It is hard to describe the actions of the shooter, a former student of the school, as anything other than the worst of what humans can do.

I first learned about the shooting at Covenant from the emails I received from my kids' schools. Covenant is equidistant between the two schools my three older children attend. The schools are well prepared for responding to shootings since it is an all too frequent occurrence in the United States. The emails read to the effect of "we have learned of an ongoing shooting at a nearby school and we are operating under Code Red. We have practiced this drill many times with the students and we are in lockdown." Michelle and I did not know what was happening, but we quickly realized that our children were safe in their schools. As the news broke, we could not—and still cannot—imagine what pain the families of the innocent victims experienced, nor the anguish and fear other parents and caregivers experienced as they waited nearby hoping to be reunited with their children.

We felt (and were) ill prepared to explain to our oldest children (who had just turned eight and six) what had happened. It was easier for us to praise how brave the police officers were (including, among others, Officers Collazo and Engelbert) and how much we appreciate teachers and those who work in schools (not only the teachers and staff at Covenant, but the teachers and staff at nearby schools who stopped their teaching duties to serve as guardians of our city's children), but we struggled to explain why a woman who lived less than half a mile from our house would choose to do something as horrific as she did.

In the days that followed, the mood in Nashville was somber. Teachers at school drop off were not smiling as they usually were, but instead looked physically pained and exhausted by the events. The demands of teachers today go far beyond simply educating our children; their responsibility to teach somehow means they are also expected to keep our children safe, including in the event of a shooting. Messages of support appeared all over the city, and flowers and other tributes were placed at the then heavily guarded entrance to the school.

The day following the shooting, Tennessee Governor Bill Lee released a video statement discussing the events at Covenant School. Describing what happened as "a tragedy beyond comprehension," Governor Lee went on to say, "Yesterday, while we saw the worst of humanity, we also saw the best of humanity in the police officers who ran into danger, directly toward a killer with no regard for their own life thinking only about those kids, those teachers, those administrators." In one day and in one single place, the best and worst of humanity were both present and on display. The events of March 27, 2023 at Covenant School showed the extreme ranges of good and terrible human behaviors.

Even in less extreme situations, humans have the potential and the ability to improve the human experience, to do good for others and the world. When our human needs are met and we can help ensure our fellow humans have the freedom and means to live with their human needs met, we feel good about humanity and what we can do, individually and collectively.

Yet, despite our ability and potential to do good, we also have the ability and potential to harm others. When left unregulated, our human ability and potential can reflect the best and worst of humanity and everything in between. The vast majority of us seek to be and see ourselves as good humans, but our intent and impact are not always one and the same. The desire to be good humans can drive us—whether for our own benefit or others'—forward, and we can struggle at times to reconcile when our acts or omissions do not align with our intent to do good. Our intelligence and our desire to feel belonging and conformity with social and group norms, to preserve and advance our sense of esteem and our desire that others see us as good incline us to justify our actions to uphold our identity as good humans or to excuse our actions when we know our behavior is wrong.

To be human is to have the needs of other human beings. To be humane is to recognize that our human needs can be met without necessarily impeding on the needs of others and even to seek ways to align our (individual and collective) identity as "good humans" with our behavior in reality. Like many other games, the game of life is best played when we have appropriate rules in place that are consistently and fairly applied. Whether those rules are social or cultural norms, government rules, or obligations imposed by organizations, **well-designed rules can help us all to live lives in which our physiological, security-based, and other needs are continuously met.**

Humans need Ethics and Compliance to support our human needs and also because we recognize the great care and responsibility with which we must exert our potential as a species. The ethics and compliance function is about humans—and helping humans use their ability and potential for good. **Ethics and compliance ultimately can help us to be humans with humanity in our workplaces, communities, and the world at large.**

When we have an ethics and compliance function that places the human experience and human needs as its purpose, we give ourselves and each other the opportunity to enjoy the human experience and to ensure that the power of human potential leads to good outcomes that are achieved in a humane way.

ADAM BALFOUR

CHAPTER 1

"PLEASE ACKNOWLEDGE THAT YOU HAVE READ AND UNDERSTOOD THIS CHAPTER"

As someone who has picked up a book on ethics and compliance, I will assume that you, the reader, are someone who views themselves as a compliant person and who follows rules and instructions. Perhaps you are so compliant in nature that you work in ethics and compliance, the legal profession, or a similar field. As such, you know the importance of compliance and, no doubt, you demonstrate compliant behavior at all times and in everything you do.

To confirm your unwavering level of compliance, I would like to ask you two fairly simple, straightforward questions. The answer to both is either "yes" or "no." The first question is: **"Have you bought, leased, or come into possession of a car within the last five years?"** This could be a new car, a pre-owned vehicle, or a vehicle you were generously gifted by someone else. Remember, your answer to this question (and the following one) should either be "yes" or "no."

The second question is: **"Did you read your car manual in its entirety before you drove your car for the first time?"**

I like to ask these questions in trainings—both for compliance professionals and for other human beings—by asking for a show of hands and watching the response. Usually, a number of hands will go up in response to the first question. Often, the hands are raised somewhat nervously since the participants suspect the question is too easy and that they must be walking into some type of trap. I then confirm their suspicions by asking those people to keep their hands raised if they have read their car manual in its entirety before they drove their car for the first time. I have yet to ask this second question in a live training and have a single hand remain raised. (I should note that some, but not all, car manuals do include a statement instructing the new car owner to read the car manual in its entirety before operating the vehicle for the first time). In full transparency, I have never read a car manual in its entirety, and unless cars change dramatically in the future, I doubt I ever will.

Does failing to read our car manuals make us reckless, uncaring, and bad drivers? Not in my opinion. Not reading your car manual in its entirety does not make you a bad driver or a bad person; it is simply a reflection that you are a human and that lengthy manuals are not the most effective way to connect with or influence the behavior of humans. Car manuals—like ethics and compliance programs— are intended to help humans, but they rarely have the desired impact because they fail to engage us as human beings.

Humans are unique and special. We are an intelligent species with the potential and ability to do incredible things. We can process complex and complicated concepts through our rational and logical intelligence to drive innovations that challenge what was possible or even imaginable in the past. Our sociability and empathy lead us to strive for more than self-preservation; through our actions today, we can help meet others' needs, including those physically or emotionally close to us, strangers in other parts of the world, and even future generations.

Despite our individual and collective potential to do good, we can—and do— cause harm to others and to the earth. Humans need freedom, but we also need guidance and regulation for our behaviors to avoid causing harm. The ethics and compliance function services that function: to guide and regulate human behaviors in ways that are effective and reflective of how we live as humans. But we must recognize that while humans can write policies, it does not necessarily mean that humans will read those policies or comply with them.

I have been incredibly fortunate to work in the ethics and compliance community for several years now. Like many others who work in ethics and

" *People are not robots who will always do as they are told. As humans, we are complex creatures with a blend of rational, irrational, logical, and emotional thoughts and responses. We're not always predictable or consistent. So when we build ethics and compliance programs with this in mind, we stand a much better chance of helping other human beings do the right thing.* "

compliance, it was not an area that I ever aspired to work in. The notion of running an ethics and compliance program seemed like a punishment—or so I thought at the time. It sounded about as fun as reading a car manual in its entirety and then trying to make sure that everyone else in the organization read and acted in accordance with their car manuals too. I have since learned that ethics and compliance programs have a terrible brand, but the brand does not reflect what ethics and compliance programs are really about, nor the full value they offer (and the brand certainly does not reflect the value of the many wonderful ethics and compliance professionals, who regularly make a positive difference for their organizations and the people those organizations impact).

What I have learned over the years is that an ethics and compliance program is not about complying with the law; it's about getting your organization's employees and other human beings to act in a way that ensures the organization complies with the law. People—whether they are your organization's employees, contractors, customers, or suppliers—are, or should be, at the heart of your ethics and compliance program because they (and not the legal entity) are the ones who do the actual compliance (or noncompliance). We have to see ethics and compliance through a people-focused lens (rather than vice versa) if we want our ethics and compliance programs to actually work in practice.

Ethics and compliance programs are about people. People are not robots who will always do as they are told. As humans, we are complex creatures with a blend of rational, irrational, logical, and emotional thoughts and responses. We're not always predictable or consistent. So when we build ethics and compliance programs with this in mind, we stand a much better chance of helping other human beings do the right thing.

We also must design ethics and compliance programs with humans in mind to protect people from harm and to make sure that those who are harmed, or who are even at risk of harm, feel comfortable to speak up and assured that their stories are heard. Ultimately, we need ethics and compliance programs for humans. We need programs that connect with humans in human ways. We connect with and are influenced by other humans and their stories far more than we connect with policies (or car manuals).

This book explains the value of effective ethics and compliance programs and offers guidance on what an effective ethics and compliance program for humans looks like in practice. This is not intended as a blueprint that you can apply to every organization, but it provides a range of ideas and approaches that can be adapted and applied based on the people in your organization, how your organization operates, and your industry.

CHAPTER 2

GREAT PRODUCT, TERRIBLE BRAND

Ask any employee in your organization what they think of when they hear "ethics and compliance program" and you are likely to hear some perceptions and experiences demonstrating that the "brand" is similar to insurance. You need to have it, but it's hard to get excited about it.

Great products with terrible brands either do not sell or do not sell as well as they could. Conversely, an appealing brand can help increase sales, and brand bias can cause us to pick a particular product over another without even thinking about it. For example, store brand medicines usually contain the same ingredients as name brands and are just as safe and effective, but they tend to differ significantly in price. There are rational reasons to pick the cheaper option, but many of us will reach for the brand-name product because we have the perception that the store brand is somehow inferior.

A brand's strength is often in how it is perceived, and its success is measured by its ability to draw you in to buy the product or otherwise take some action. If a company invests heavily in its marketing efforts and nobody buys the product or service being offered, then there might be strong "brand awareness," but not much else. That's why measuring whether or not someone is aware of a brand reveals little value to the brand owner; nor does this measurement indicate how people feel toward the brand and whether they are likely to interact with its products or services—by spending their money, time, or both. Just look at Enron, Lehman Brothers, and Arthur Andersen. Those companies still have brands many people are aware of, but that brand awareness has little to no value at this point.

Your ethics and compliance programs have a brand. The question is whether the perception employees and others have of the brand is favorable, reflecting the value your program provides, and whether you've done anything to intentionally manage that brand.

For example, many well-intentioned organizations repeatedly remind employees that they have a code of conduct and an ethics and compliance program. I have even heard of several companies measuring and tracking what percentage of employees know that the code of conduct exists. These efforts certainly make people aware of the code of conduct and the program, but this tactic alone falls far short of "brand management." Measuring whether employees are aware of your code of conduct does nothing to reveal whether anyone has actually read it or understood it, nor whether they find it useful.

Scott Bedbury is a branding consultant and expert. He has helped to transform the brands of some of the biggest global companies, contributing to Nike's "Just Do It" campaign and Starbucks' marketing efforts to be seen as the "third place" (behind home and work). Bedbury's 2002 book, A New Brand World: Eight Principles for Achieving Brand Leadership in the Twenty-First Century,[1] significantly changed how I approach ethics and compliance. Bedbury explains that for a long time, companies measured the success of their marketing and branding efforts by brand awareness; however, Bedbury shares that branding has moved on from this approach since "[r]elying on brand awareness has become marketing fool's gold." He explains that focusing on brand relevance and brand resonance are far more important and useful measurements: "brand relevance and brand resonance [are] two measures of brand strength that are much more valuable than mere brand awareness can ever be. Perhaps this is the greatest change in the concept of 'brand' in recent years. Where we once looked at brands on a surface level, we now view them in more intimate and multidimensional terms."

And since we're talking about branding, I'll take a moment to quote myself from an article I wrote for CEP Magazine, which now owns the copyright to

---

[1] Scott Bedbury and Stephen Fenichell, *A New Brand World: Eight Principles for Achieving Brand Leadership in the Twenty-First Century* (New York: Penguin Books, 2002).

that material. (I respect copyright laws—and I want to stay on the good side of the Society of Corporate Compliance and Ethics and CEP Magazine in hopes of writing more articles for them in the future):

"Making your compliance program relevant and resonate with employees is not easy and will require investments of time, creative and mental energy, and perhaps some money, but the return on investment is worth it. If we want to have an effective compliance program, we must learn how to leverage the branding concepts of brand relevance and resonance to truly connect with and engage employees." [2]

At this point you might be thinking, "Is brand management really part of my job description?" You might be feeling some resistance to expanding the definition of your current role—especially if you come from a legal background. After all, aren't ethics and compliance programs all about laws, rules, and regulations? We'll talk more about that later, believe me. For now, trust me when I say I did not learn anything about "brand management" at law school. And while my legal background helps in various aspects of my role, I have learned that I cannot simply "think like a lawyer" when managing the perception of ethics and compliance programs or communicating their value to employees.

Right now is a good time to address the eternal question: **Do you need to have a law degree or a legal background to work in ethics and compliance?** Some people will disagree with me, but I say the answer is a definite "no."Having a legal background helps me in some aspects of my job, but the legal lens often provides too narrow a view for ethics and compliance issues. There is a lot more to building and running an effective ethics and compliance program than just knowing the law, especially if your goal is to challenge the common (and inaccurate) perception that compliance is simply a rules-based discipline.

It's hard to get people excited about an ethics and compliance program if your only argument for having one is "regulators expect us to" or "so we avoid our

---

[2] Adam Balfour, "Leveraging branding concepts to drive an effective compliance program," *CEP Magazine*, June 2021, https://compliancecosmos.org/leveraging-branding-concepts-drive-effective-compliance-program

CEO going to jail and us getting fined." Ethics and compliance are ultimately about human behavior, which is why seeing people only through a legal- or rules-based lens is ineffective and misses the bigger picture.

Ethics and compliance professionals may often be lawyers, but they also must be leaders, marketers, behavioral scientists, negotiators, HR investigators, and public speakers. They also must operate as humans themselves. A multidisciplinary, curious, and innovative mindset is more valuable than a particular (or even any) degree.

If you have more than one person on the ethics and compliance team, then you can become stronger by leveraging the combined knowledge, skills, and experience of each person. But even if your team is small (or if you are a "team of one"), you can develop and hone the skills you need to manage your brand.

Ethics and compliance for humans is about connecting with people, helping them, and demonstrating that they are what ethics and compliance is about. So put on your marketing hat and get ready to address some negative brand perceptions in Chapter 3.

ADAM BALFOUR

CHAPTER 3

THE DIRTY DOZEN: ADDRESSING 12 NEGATIVE BRAND PERCEPTIONS TO HUMANIZE YOUR E&C PROGRAM

By leaning into some of the assumptions people have about ethics and compliance, we can begin to improve our programs and intentionally change the brand perception. In this chapter, we will consider and address some of what I consider to be the most commonly held assumptions. These misperceptions are often held by employees outside of the ethics and compliance function and, sometimes, by those within it.

#1. ETHICS AND COMPLIANCE ARE ABOUT LAWS, RULES, AND REGULATIONS.

Sometimes rules or standards are established externally to your organization (by a regulatory body, for example), and other times the rules or standards are established within your organization (to help ensure compliance with externally imposed standards, to address risks facing the organization, to advance organizational values or, candidly, as a function of bureaucracy). Rules and standards are certainly relevant and important to an ethics and compliance program, but people tend to see ethics and compliance programs only through a rules-focused lens. And that's a problem.

Consider the role of rules in sports: The rules are there to ensure the game is played competitively, safely, fairly, and consistently. Rules also protect the interests of various stakeholders (the players or athletes, the sport's governing body, the officials, the team owners, the fans). The rules of one sport are not necessarily going to work for another sport (imagine trying to apply the rules of tennis to boxing, for example), and many people who know the rules learned them by watching the sport or playing the game rather than regularly reading a rule book. Rules are indeed important to a sport, but are the rules themselves the ultimate purpose or objective of the game?

Laws, rules, and regulations are not the ultimate purpose of a compliance and ethics program, either. They help ensure that the "infinite game" (in the words of Simon Sinek) of business is played competitively, safely, fairly, and consistently— and to help protect the interests of various stakeholders. stakeholders. (employees, shareholders, directors, customers, and other business partners).

Despite our efforts to think we are training employees through the rule-following actions of completing online courses or reviewing written policies (including check-the-box certifications to the effect of "I have read and understood the attached policy and understand that noncompliance on my part could result in disciplinary proceedings up to and including termination of my employment"), most employees learn from "playing the game." That is, they learn the rules by doing their jobs, interacting with other people, and seeing what behaviors are tolerated, rewarded, and punished in the organization.

Rules are important to ethics and compliance programs, but people are the purpose.

#2. POLICIES AND PROGRAMS THAT WORK FOR ONE ORGANIZATION WILL WORK FOR ANOTHER.

Have you ever tried to get around Paris with a map of New York? ? The absurdity of such a plan is similar to trying to take an ethics and compliance program that works for one organization and apply it to another. You cannot simply "copy and paste" a program that is designed for and works well in one organization and expect it to have the same result in a different organization. For example, an ethics and compliance program that is designed for and effective in a less-regulated, low-risk organization will not be suitable, appropriately designed, or

" . . . *most employees learn from "playing the game." That is, they learn the rules by doing their jobs, interacting with other people, and seeing what behaviors are tolerated, rewarded, and punished in the organization.* **"**

effective in practice if it is simply applied to a highly regulated business that has global operations and a significantly higher risk profile.

An organization's ethics and compliance program and code of conduct should be your organization's "ethical map," giving direction to your employees about your organization's ethical values and principles, addressing the applicable laws, and helping your employees to navigate the potentially difficult or ethically murky situations they may encounter in your organization. While there is a lot to be learned by benchmarking and looking at ethics and compliance programs of other organizations, you cannot simply copy the ethics and compliance program of another organization or create generic or off-the-shelf policies.

Another example to illustrate this point is when an organization has a policy that addresses the giving or receiving of gifts, meals, entertainment, or travel to or from third parties. While some gift-giving can violate laws (for instance, if you are giving or offering an item of value to try to bribe or unduly influence someone), other gift-giving is not regulated by law, but instead set by an organization's values and business approach. In some instances, companies may say that they do not want to engage in this type of behavior for whatever reason (perhaps to ensure that pricing is as competitive as it can be without factoring in the cost of wining and dining and other expenses considered unnecessary). In other instances, gift-giving and social interactions with third parties can be considered acceptable and even aligned with the organization's overall purpose and strategy (e.g., an organization in the hospitality business wanting to demonstrate the hospitable services it offers).

There simply is no off-the-shelf template that can be downloaded and rolled out. Designing and building a program that will work for your organization requires an understanding of the organization's purpose, strategies, brand, and ethical values.

#3. AN EFFECTIVE PROGRAM MEETS THE EXPECTATIONS OF REGULATORS. DOING MORE IS UNNECESSARY AND COSTLY.

Ethics and compliance professionals often discuss having—or wanting to have—a "best-in-class" program, which I think can leave people wondering what that even means or how a "best-in-class" program is more desirable or beneficial.

I often see parallels between my professional life and my personal life as the parent of four young children. Think about the following question: *How would you describe a "best-in-class" parent or caregiver?* My guess is that many of us would describe such a caregiver in the following ways:

- Shows genuine love and care.

- Willing and able to help a child learn and grow. This might mean challenging them to venture outside their comfort zone, but in a way that is safe.

- Looks out for risks and determines which risks could have significant consequences for the child. Conducts ongoing risk assessments that evolve as the child ages.

- Takes appropriate steps to prevent the occurrence or impact of such risks. This could be as simple as assessing the safety of a playground, overseeing a child trying to do things beyond their ever-changing abilities, monitoring environmental factors such as inclement weather or having other children around, and assessing whether they are close enough to help the child if needed.

- Helps children learn about values and to behave and to uphold those values and expected standards.

- Creates a level of trust so the child feels it is safe to speak up when they have problems or concerns and knows they will be listened to when they do.

Obviously this isn't an exhaustive list. There are many other caregiver traits we should aspire and live up to. However, I don't think anyone would say that a "best-in-class" caregiver is one who simply meets expectations or satisfies the minimal standards set by law. While child welfare services have valid interests in protecting children, the legal standards set to protect children are (hopefully) viewed by many as being the minimum standard, one that we all aspire to—and, in fact, do—significantly exceed.

When we see ethics and compliance as being about and for people, we see that the standards of regulators (such as the United States Department of Justice, the United States Securities and Exchange Commission, and the many other regulatory bodies around the world) do not necessarily define the "golden" or maximum standard of what we should aspire to achieve. If our ethics and compliance programs only focus on "not getting fined" or "keeping our executives out of jail," then we fail to create and deliver the value that a human-centric ethics and compliance program can deliver.

#4. ETHICS AND COMPLIANCE PROGRAMS ARE ONLY ABOUT AVOIDING FINES AND PENALTIES FOR THE ORGANIZATION.

While corporations and other organizations can be found liable for wrongdoing, the entity itself does not do the wrongdoing; it is the people acting on the entity's behalf whose actions (or inactions, as the case may be) result in wrongdoing and liability. That's why people—whether your organization's employees, contractors, or others—must be at the heart of your ethics and compliance program. They, and not the legal entity, are the ones who actually achieve compliance (or fail to).

This does not mean we can forget or diminish the risk and financial impact of potential fines and penalties, but we can more effectively manage that risk by engaging the people whose behavior can help manage, mitigate, or amplify the risks and consequences of noncompliance.

A corporate compliance program is, therefore, not about merely complying with the law to avoid fines; it is about getting your organization's employees (and any other humans who act on behalf of the organization) to act in a way that will ensure the organization complies with the law.

It is not uncommon now to see penalties and fines for ethics and compliance violations in the billions of dollars. Beyond the damage to financial results and cash flows, fines and penalties can impact an organization's share price.

"If you think that compliance is expensive, try noncompliance."
— U.S. Deputy AG Paul McNulty

While an effective ethics and compliance program reduces the likelihood of financial losses and reputation-damaging headlines, the goal is far broader than simply "avoiding bad things." Ethics and compliance programs add significant value to an organization's bottom line, and there is a growing amount of data that supports this.

- Ethisphere, which compiles an annual list of the World's Most Ethical Companies, found that the most ethical companies had a "five-year ethics premium" and "outperformed a comparable index of large cap companies by 13.6 percentage points from January 2018 to January 2023."[3]

- Simon Webley and Elise More, authors of "Does Business Ethics Pay?," found that "companies with 'an ethical culture' outperformed those that made no such claims in three important financial measures: (1) market value added; (2) economic value added; and (3) price/earnings ratio." [4]

- A 2018 article in the Harvard Business Review stated that "whistleblowers—and large numbers of them—are crucial to keeping

[3] Ethisphere, "2023 World's Most Ethical Companies," March 2023, https://ethisphere.com/ethisphere-announces-the-2023-worlds-most-ethical-companies/.
[4] Simon Webley and Elise More, *Does Business Ethics Pay?* (Institute of Business Ethics, 2003)

firms healthy and that functioning internal hotlines are of paramount importance to business goals including profitability." The authors went on to quantify some of the many benefits of whistleblowers (I do not particularly like the term "whistleblower" and think the value of people who speak up is better captured by Dr. Catherine A. Sanderson's moniker "moral rebels" or my own preferred term, "people who care," which is explained in greater detail in Chapter 5), which include 6.9% fewer pending lawsuits and 20.4% smaller aggregate settlement amounts. Additionally, according to the authors' findings, organizations "that are more active in using their [internal reporting] systems tend to be more profitable (as measured by return on assets) than firms that are less active users of their systems." [5]

---

[5] Stephen Stubben and Kyle Welch, "Research: Whistleblowers Are a Sign of Healthy Companies," *Harvard Business Review,* November 2018, https://hbr.org/2018/11/research-whistleblowers-are-a-sign-of-healthy-companies.

In 2016, the **U.S. Department of Justice** announced that two Brazilian companies, **Odebrecht S.A.** (now known as Novonor) and **Braskem, S.A.**, would pay "at least $3.5 billion in global penalties to resolve the largest foreign bribery case in history." In 2020, the DOJ announced that **Airbus** had agreed to "pay over $3.9 billion in global penalties" for bribery. In 2022, **Google** was fined over €4.1 billion for antitrust violations. While **Walmart's** $282 million fine in 2019 for bribery by its Brazilian business unit might pale in comparison, it is estimated that "Walmart wound up spending about $1 billion in legal fees and other costs related to the investigation" (the investigation lasted seven years).

Luckin Coffee, founded in 2017, is a coffeehouse chain in China that quickly grew in terms of store locations and its ability to compete against **Starbucks** in China. In 2019, Luckin Coffee became a publicly traded company on the **Nasdaq** stock exchange when its stock sold for $17 a share, and market confidence continued to grow as the company's share price reached over $50 a share by January 2020. However, following revelations of an accounting scandal involving sales fraud that resulted in the CEO and COO being fired and the company receiving a delisting notice from the Nasdaq, Luckin Coffee's share price plummeted to $1.39 per share (the company was also later fined $180 million by the **U.S. Securities and Exchange Commission** and filed for bankruptcy).

Although Luckin Coffee has since emerged from bankruptcy proceedings and its share price has recovered a lot of value, it is still trading far below the January 2020 high of $50 a share.

#5. ETHICAL, HONEST PEOPLE DON'T NEED ETHICS AND COMPLIANCE PROGRAMS; E&C PROGRAMS ARE FOR CATCHING THE SMALL NUMBER OF PEOPLE WHO COMMIT HARM.

Most of us see ourselves as ethical and compliant people, and our actions are often consistent with that identity. However, our identity and actions can sometimes be at odds with one another. Our thinking and behavior are often influenced by the pressures we face and the social norms of the groups to which we belong. This does not mean that an effective program should treat everyone as a potential criminal, but we must address humans' susceptibility to pressure and help people ensure that their acts both align with their identity and are compliant with the relevant standards.

In February 2020, the U.S. Department of Justice announced that Wells Fargo had "agreed to pay $3 billion to resolve their potential criminal and civil liability stemming from a practice between 2002 and 2016 of pressuring employees to meet unrealistic sales goals that led thousands of employees to provide millions of accounts or products to customers under false pretenses or without consent." As then-current U.S. Attorney Nick Hanna for the Central District of California said, "this case illustrates a complete failure of leadership at multiple levels within the Bank." This was not one or two individuals who "went rogue;" this was literally thousands of people who were aware and were no doubt influenced less by company policy than by the words and actions of peers and leaders, the company culture, and the objectives they had been tasked (and pressured, and incentivized) to achieve.

Pressure is not inherently bad. The right type and amount of pressure can help us, both individually and collectively, achieve more than we would otherwise. Pressure can motivate us and provide benefits, including good outcomes. But unchecked pressure or pressure to achieve results at the expense of ethics, the law, and the legitimate interests of ourselves and others can wreak havoc on an organization, its culture, its people, and society in general.

A 2020 Global Business Ethics Survey published by the Ethics & Compliance Initiative found that "globally, more than 1 in every 5 employees feel pressure to compromise their organization's ethics standards, policies, or the law" and that pressure was felt by a higher percentage of people in North America (31%) and South America (37%).[6] That is a disturbingly large number of people who are feeling pressure to compromise standards that should never be compromised.

We need to remember: Not all humans are bad or untrustworthy. But not all humans, including and especially those of us who identify ourselves as being of strong moral character, will always do the expected or right thing. Christian Hunt, a former regulator and chief compliance officer who is also one of the most engaging speakers on compliance and behavioral science, wrote in his recent book, Humanizing Risk, that "people are people" and that "every single one of us . . . makes mistakes, breaks laws, circumvents rules, and tells lies. Not all of the time, of course . . . But sometimes—probably more often than we might like to admit—we will." People are indeed people, and we can design our programs to help people do the right thing and to support them in ensuring that their actions are aligned with their ethical identity.

#6. EMPLOYEES WHO CERTIFY THEY HAVE READ AND UNDERSTOOD POLICIES HAVE ACTUALLY READ THE POLICIES.

As a lawyer, I always review in detail the terms and conditions my client is agreeing to; however, I will readily admit that I do not adopt the same level of scrutiny when it comes to my own purchases and transactions. If my phone or an app I use asks me to check a box to confirm that "I have read and understood the terms and conditions of the End User License Agreement," I readily check the box and get on with my day. There is no room to negotiate the terms and conditions, and check-the-box gates are a point of pain impeding my progress; I can either go through the pain of actually reading some legalese document that will inevitably reveal how one-sided the terms are, or I can check the box without having read the terms and take what I assume are fairly minimal risks.

---

[6] "Pressure in the Workplace: Possible Risk Factors and Those at Risk," Global Business Ethics Survey, 2020, https://www.ethics.org/wp-content/uploads/2020_1-GBES-Pressure-in-the-Workplace-FINAL.pdf

It is common for ethics and compliance programs to ask employees at various times to acknowledge that they have read and understood certain policies and confirm their future compliance with the terms. From a defensive standpoint, I understand why organizations do this; however, anyone who believes that a 100% acknowledgement rate means that 100% acknowledgement of those employees have actually read and understood the policy is kidding themselves (and they are kidding themselves and their Board of Directors if they proudly report this as a metric or data point to the board). If your organization feels the need to include a certification box, it is more human and realistic to include a certification that reads "I have received a copy of the policy or it has otherwise been made available to me and been provided with the opportunity to read the policy. I agree to comply with the policy whether or not I have chosen to read it."

A paper published in October 2022 questioned whether or not policies (regardless of length) have any impact on employee behavior.[7] Policies are simply written standards and are often not reflective of the actual standards that are tolerated and promoted by the day-to-day activities of an organization, including who rises to the top, who stays where they are, and who is asked—or forced—to leave the organization. A certification from every employee that says they have read and understood all written policies is fairly meaningless if the expected and permitted standards in reality are different from the written policies. I am not advocating for the end of policy certifications, but only that we should be realistic and honest about what this approach actually does and not rely on it too heavily.

#7. ZERO-TOLERANCE POLICIES ARE MOST EFFECTIVE.

Policies that include zero-tolerance statements are often well-intentioned in communicating that certain behaviors will not be allowed, but good intentions do not always result in good consequences. Zero-tolerance policies are often ineffective when inconsistently enforced and also because (as an EEOC task

---

[7] Nils Köbis, Sharon Oded, Anne Leonore de Bruijn, Shuyu Huang, Benjamin van Rooij, "Is Less More? Field Evidence on the Impact of Anti-bribery Policies on Employee Knowledge and Corrupt Behavior" SSRN (October 21, 2022), https://ssrn.com/abstract=4255148.

> ### PRINTED CODES OF CONDUCT ARE ABOUT AS WELL READ AS PRINTED AIRPLANE SAFETY INSTRUCTIONS
>
> My "mini-me" recently read the airplane safety instructions on a spring break ski trip because it was something new for him while he was bored before takeoff. I didn't see any adults reading the safety instructions (myself included), yet every seat had a printed copy. Printed policies and mundane trainings might be what everyone has "always" done, but it doesn't mean they always work or are effective. It is absolutely key to make sure employees understand the relevant standards applicable to their role, but there are many ways beyond printed policies and mundane trainings to achieve that result. This is another reason to shift mindsets from "training and communication" to "learning and engagement,"as I will discuss in Chapter 6. Focus on the desired and actual impact on the target audience and find effective ways to get to that outcome, rather than focusing only on the "traditional" approaches and hoping for the desired outcome.

force commented in 2016) they can lead to underreporting "particularly where they [the employee being subjected to workplace harassment] do not want a colleague or co-worker to lose their job over relatively minor harassing behavior—they simply want the harassment to stop."

Zero-tolerance policies that focus on automatic consequences for wrongdoers (e.g., termination of employment) are not always effective in achieving their objective and run a real risk of underreporting. (often, the people who are subject to inappropriate or harmful behavior simply want the behavior to stop but don't necessarily want the offender to lose their job and income). In contrast, zero-tolerance policies that focus on behaviors are likely to be more effective and can better support victims of wrongdoing who simply want the wrongdoing to stop.

Sometimes wrongdoing can be effectively and fairly addressed and stopped through feedback and coaching or other measures short of termination; a hard-line, zero-tolerance stance that focuses on the person rather than the behavior does not allow for that. There will still be occasions when the wrongdoer should be fired (and hopefully they will be fired in those instances), but such decisions should be made thoughtfully—not necessarily automatically—after assessing the particular circumstances. A people-centric approach allows organizations to be tough on behaviors that there is zero tolerance for while taking a fair and thoughtful approach to all the relevant people involved and in light of the organization's values.

#8. ETHICS AND COMPLIANCE TRAINING WORKS.

For many organizations, one of the key pillars of the ethics and compliance program is titled "training and communications." This is understandable, since the phrase "training and communications" is used by the Department of Justice in the Evaluation of Corporate Compliance Programs. I advocate changing the mindset from "training and communication" to "learning and engagement" to ensure that our focus is less on the intent of training and communication efforts and more on the actual impact on the target audience. Did they learn what they needed to learn? Were they engaged? Did the relevant content resonate with them? The whole purpose of training and communication is to ultimately influence human behavior and thinking, so it makes more sense to focus on whether our efforts are actually helping engage people and on supporting them in learning what they need to know for their role.

Helping people learn is an important element of an effective ethics and compliance program; however, training and learning alone are rarely enough to ensure people do the right thing in the moment.

In most places, it is illegal to use your phone while you are driving (unless you are using it "hands free"). While the dangers and legality of texting and driving are well-known (new drivers are trained on this during driving lessons and tested on it during the exam), too many people continue to text and drive (I recall seeing someone driving through the crosswalk in my neighborhood a few years ago, typing on a full-sized tablet device resting against the steering wheel). We know the dangers—both to ourselves and others and of being caught—yet many people of all ages and walks of life continue to text while driving. Training alone cannot counter the effects of isolated decision-making *("I am at a stop light or driving slowly, so this is probably okay" or "I just need to send a quick email since I am running late")*. This is also what Daniel Kahneman describes in his book, Thinking, Fast And Slow, as regression to the mean; training or feedback might have a short-term impact, but we regress to our default or "mean" average position shortly afterwards.

As someone who is (a) constantly on his phone and (b) knows the importance of safe driving, I, candidly, do not trust myself with my phone in my car. I understand the temptation of reaching for your phone at a stop light or other similar situation where utilitarian thinking using isolated decision-making could cause me to go against my better judgment and the standards expected of drivers. Trying to balance these competing interests can be tricky and challenging in the moment, so I have found that using technology can help. My phone is set up with "Driving Focus" always turned on, which means my phone automatically senses when I am driving and automatically goes into locked mode. Anyone who calls will be sent to voicemail, and anyone who sends a text message will receive an auto-reply message indicating that reads "I'm driving with Do Not Disturb While Driving turned on so I can focus on driving and not get distracted by my phone.

I won't be able to see or reply to your message until I get to where I'm going." By automatically disabling my ability to use my phone (it still allows navigation and audio to play), the temptation is neutralized and I can focus my attention on driving (and occasionally berating other drivers who I see on their phones).

I share this example to make the point that while technology cannot replace common sense, nor can we rely on it completely as our only protection, it actually can help to maintain standards that were part of past training and learning. Most ethics and compliance training also target what Daniel Kahneman calls our "System 2" thinking, which is more deliberate, rational, and controlled thinking; however, we need to find ways to support and supplement our "System 1" thinking. Our System 1 thinking is our fast thinking, which is often driven by our automatic responses and accounts for the majority of the thinking we do in our fast-paced world where we are bombarded by multiple, simultaneous demands for our attention and focus.

Helping people learn is indeed a key hallmark of an effective ethics and compliance program, but we can and should supplement training and learning with technology, controls, and culture to ensure that what we are meant to do is what we actually do in practice. Thankfully, we are seeing an increase in the amount, quality, and usefulness of ethics and compliance-related technology—tools that actually help people stay aligned with the standards they were trained on—and we need to continue pressing for the evolution and adoption of this technology. Human-centric training coupled with technology that helps in the moment can help each of us to live up to the standards expected of us.

#9. A HEALTHY CULTURE IS ONE WHERE THERE ARE NO ETHICS HOTLINE REPORTS.

I often get asked *"Isn't the goal to have zero reports through the ethics hotline or through other speak-up channels? Doesn't having reports suggest there are issues, and don't you want to have no issues"?* I think this is a completely valid question, and I appreciate the candor when someone asks it. The answer is "yes and no."

I agree: It would be ideal if there were no issues that needed to be raised. That would be wonderful and, if it were the case, having no reports through the hotline or any other speak-up channel would be a good thing. In the same way, it would be great if the police did not get reports of crime because no crime was occurring, or if doctors, nurses, and other medical professionals could find less stressful career options or work shorter and less stressful shifts because nobody ever gets sick or requires medical treatment. However, we do not live in a utopian world where nothing bad ever happens. The reality is, just as we will always have a need for law enforcement and medical professionals, we will always have issues and questionable behavior in the workplace that impacts other humans. We are better off if we hear and know about those issues so they can be addressed.

While many ethics and compliance programs look at metrics such as "number of reports per 100 employees" as a way to benchmark performance internally and against other organizations, this is not always an accurate indicator of whether relevant issues are being raised. We need to consider what issues are being raised, what issues are occurring but not being raised, what the experience is of those who speak up, and whether the speak-up process is actually helping the people, values, and performance of the organization. A culture of psychological safety that supports people speaking up will also lend itself well to people feeling safer to be more creative, strive for excellence (rather fear failure), and genuinely be their true selves in the workplace.

#10. BEWARE OF ENCOURAGING TOO MUCH SPEAKING UP. PEOPLE WILL INVENT ISSUES, RAISE TRIVIAL MATTERS, OR USE THE HOTLINE TO COMPLAIN ABOUT THE CAFETERIA FOOD.

As much as we might want to admit it, we all lie, and we do it a lot more frequently than we likely care to admit. According to Dopamine Nation by Anna Lembke, the average person will tell between 0.59 and 1.56 lies per day.[8]

---

[8] Anna Lembke, *Dopamine Nation: Finding Balance in the Age of Indulgence* (n.p.: 2021).

(How this was measured is a mystery to me.) That being said, I have yet to come across any data that suggests that encouraging employees to speak up will result in a material increase of knowingly false reports made to the hotline or any other speak-up channel. If you are properly conducting investigations based on the allegations raised, then you can (a) likely weed out any reports not raised in good faith, since there will be a lack of evidence to support such false allegations, and (b) track metrics such as your substantiation rates to understand if something is going on that suggests employees may need training or other appropriate efforts.

From time to time, employees may raise matters that appear to be very minor or trivial in the grand scheme of things. However, an issue that appears small or insignificant from the organization's perspective can, in fact, be of huge significance to the person reporting the matter. Moreover, if several people are complaining about the food in your cafeteria, then perhaps you should have someone look into that. If the food is so bad that people are taking the time and effort to speak up, then show them you actually listen. Addressing a minor matter may help build the trust needed for your employees to speak up about matters the organization considers to be more significant. Organizations cannot directly build speak-up cultures; a speak-up culture is the product or result of the organization consistently, genuinely showing that it listens to its employees and cares about their experiences and well-being.

#11. FEAR OF RETALIATION IS THE #1 REASON EMPLOYEES DON'T SPEAK UP.

Retaliation can have a chilling effect on both the individual retaliated against and other employees who become aware of it (you do not have to do much searching to find stories of legitimate and good faith whistleblowers who have been treated horribly and the toll retaliation takes on a person). As bad as retaliation is, this is not the most common reason people cite for not speaking up, according to a Gallup report from September 2020.[9] Gallup's study, which

---

[9] Nate Dvorak and Alex Power, "Culture Drives Your Ethics and Compliance Reporting Ratio," *Gallup*, September 2, 2020, *https://www.gallup.com/workplace/318197/culture-drives-ethics-compliance-reporting-ratio.aspx*

was based on the U.S. working population, found that **26% of respondents said that the "primary reason" for not reporting breaches of ethics was because "I thought no action would be taken."** Other reasons provided included:

"I was afraid of retaliation" (21%);

"I previously reported a compliance or ethics issue, and it was not a good experience" (10%);

"I was not sure it was a violation" (9%); and

"I didn't want to get anyone in trouble." (4%)

There are, unfortunately, a number of reasons people do not speak up when they have witnessed or experienced misconduct, and it is important to understand what may keep your employees from speaking up. Employees must feel psychologically safe and that any barriers to raising issues—whether actual or perceived—are acknowledged and addressed.

#12. A CULTURE OF COMPLIANCE IS ALWAYS GOOD.

This might seem like an odd assumption to include, especially since the word "compliance" appears in the title of this book and throughout every chapter. Corporate culture is indeed important; regulators have made that clear. See, for instance, Deputy Attorney General Lisa O. Monaco's remarks in New York City on September 15, 2022: She referred to "culture" fourteen times, including the very true statement, "It all comes back to corporate culture." We can also see that the term "culture of compliance" is mentioned several times in the DOJ's "Evaluation of Corporate Compliance Programs." When people comply with the stated or expected standards, provided those standards are not immoral or otherwise unethical, such individual and collective compliance is indeed desirable and good. This is the culture of compliance that we seek and hope to attain.

However, too often we see that an organization's stated or written standards (such as those described in policies) and its actual standards are very different. Consider Enron, for example, the now bankrupt entity in which a massive accounting scandal resulted in thousands of people losing their jobs and many others taking a significant financial hit due to the Enron retirement plans tanking. Enron allegedly had "integrity," "communication," "respect," and "excellence" carved in marble at the company's headquarters in Houston, Texas. The acts of Kenneth Lay, Enron's founder, CEO, and Chairman, and many others, built a culture that was certainly not aligned with any of those stated values. There was no agreement between Enron's stated and written standards and those in practice.

While some wrongdoing does involve a single individual acting alone, there are many instances in which large groups of people are involved to varying degrees. When people are not incentivized and rewarded based on the written or stated standards, but are instead pressured and incentivized to comply with the actual standards in practice (which are inconsistent with the stated standards), a culture of compliance still exists; people are complying with the actual or implicit standards, but certainly not the stated or written standards.

I referred previously to the Wells Fargo scandal that resulted in the bank paying a $3 billion fine. Banking is a heavily regulated industry, and Wells Fargo most certainly had a formal ethics and compliance program. However, as we saw earlier, there was "a practice between 2002 and 2016 of pressuring employees to meet unrealistic sales goals that led thousands of employees to provide millions of accounts or products to customers under false pretenses or without consent." This was not one or two individuals who "went rogue" or were "bad apples;" literally thousands of people were involved and were, no doubt, influenced less by their policies than by their peers, leaders, the culture, and the objectives they had been tasked and incentivized to achieve. Wells Fargo's ethics and compliance program on paper and its culture of compliance in practice were clearly at odds, but because of the incentives in place and the pressure leadership brought to bear, it was the culture of compliance to achieve the "unrealistic sales goals" that prevailed over the bank's stated and written ethics and compliance program.

In June 2022, Ernst & Young was fined a record $100 million after it was discovered that "a significant number of EY audit professionals cheated on the ethics component of CPA exams and various continuing professional education courses required to maintain CPA licenses, including ones designed to ensure that accountants can properly evaluate whether clients' financial statements comply with Generally Accepted Accounting Principles." [10] A statement from SEC Commissioner Hester M. Peirce stated, "Hundreds of EY personnel across multiple offices cheated over several years by, among other things, sharing answer keys and manipulating testing software... Moreover, despite an EY code of conduct requirement to report unethical conduct, many EY employees who knew of the cheating did not report it. Although the firm investigated reported misconduct and disciplined some cheaters, the cheating did not stop... In sum, there is a solid case against EY based on the widespread cheating and failure of its quality control system, and I could have supported an enforcement action and settlement focused on that conduct." [11]

An article in The Guardian quoted a statement from Ernst & Young that read "nothing is more important than our integrity and our ethics." [12] Ernst & Young clearly had a culture of compliance about its exam cheating practices that went against the standard and expected standards of its ethics and compliance

---

[10] U.S. Securities and Exchange Commission, "Ernst & Young to Pay $100 Million Penalty for Employees Cheating on CPA Ethics Exams and Misleading Investigation," June 28, 2022, https://www.sec.gov/news/press-release/2022-114.

[11] Hester M. Peirce, "When Voluntary Means Mandatory and Forever: Statement on In the Matter of Ernst & Young LLP," SEC, June 28, 2022, https://www.sec.gov/news/statement/peirce-statement-ernst-and-young-062822.

[12] Dominic Rushe, "Ernst & Young pays $100m to settle US charges of cheating on ethics exams," The Guardian, June 28, 2022, https://www.theguardian.com/business/2022/jun/28/ernst-and-young-fined-cheating-audit-settlement

program. Having a written policy in place is of little value if the actual policy in practice is completely different.

A culture of compliance is neither inherently good nor bad; it depends on what people are being asked, incentivized, and pressured to comply with. The examples of Enron, Wells Fargo, and Ernst & Young demonstrate that a culture of compliance does not always align with the ethics and compliance program. I view the term "culture of compliance" as not being particularly useful, since compliance can either be good or bad; instead, I think the term "culture of integrity" is more appropriate and useful. (For an excellent and much more detailed discussion on driving an intentional culture of integrity, I recommend Intentional Integrity: How Smart Companies Can Lead An Ethical Revolution by Rob Chesnut, former General Counsel and Chief Ethics Officer of Airbnb). The wrongdoing at Enron, Wells Fargo, and Ernst & Young, among many other examples, showed a distinct lack of a culture of integrity. In fact, the SEC's press release on Ernst & Young quoted Gurbir S. Grewal, Director of the SEC's Enforcement Division as saying, "the SEC will not tolerate integrity failures."

ADAM BALFOUR

CHAPTER 4

WHO ARE THE HUMANS WE'RE TRYING TO HELP?

I regularly reference a 2015 article in The Guardian about the Petrobras corruption scandal. The author, journalist Jonathan Watts, shared quotes from various low-paid employees and who lost their jobs because of the scandal. One quote in particular has really stuck with me: **"I'm very worried. I have a two-year-old daughter who depends on me. I'm sinking into depression. I've lost 6kg since this started."** [13]

We often don't hear these voices; they are often drowned out by other headlines relating to the scandals. Many employees depend on their jobs to provide for themselves and their loved ones, and some of them might not have much in the way of savings to get them through periods of unemployment. Regulators and enforcement agencies are important stakeholders in ensuring your organization's ethics and compliance program works well, but there are many other stakeholders—including your employees and those who rely on their income—who also have a vested interest in your organization's ethics and compliance program. The best way to show care for your organization's employees is by making sure they aren't at risk of losing their jobs as a result of a massive compliance scandal.

Speaking of scandals, does anyone love a scandal as much as a headline-writer?

"Former Bumble Bee C.E.O. Is Sentenced in Tuna Price-Fixing Scheme," The New York Times, June 16, 2020

"Ex-Braskem CEO to Plead Guilty in $250 Million Bribery Case," Bloomberg, March 30, 2021

"Hockey Canada Sex-Assault Scandal Forces Out CEO, Entire Board," Bloomberg, October 11, 2022

---

[13] Jonathan Watts, "Brazil elite profit from $3bn Petrobras scandal as laid-off workers pay the price," *The Guardian*, March 20, 2015, https://www.theguardian.com/world/2015/mar/20/brazil-petrobras-scandal-layoffs-dilma-rousseff.

These typical headlines focus on wrongdoers and their wrongdoing. But what about the victims who suffered the consequences of the wrongdoing? Focusing on the wrongdoers and the wrongdoing can show others what not to do, but these headlines tend to ignore the consequences of the wrongdoing and fail to tell the human stories of those impacted. They also do not highlight the benefit of ethical behavior.

Why do we often see a lack of focus on victims? In certain instances, some individuals may not want their identity known or to have their trauma played out in the public eye, but there can and should be an acknowledgment of the human consequences. The stories of impacted people are important and deserve consideration.

With headlines often ignoring the victims' stories and focusing on wrongdoers, it is understandable that ethics and compliance programs also tend to focus on the behavior of wrongdoers. But this approach fails to see and acknowledge the human experience of ethics and compliance.

In this chapter, we will look past the wrongdoers to consider those harmed by wrongdoing. Ethics and compliance programs can and should be designed to help these people.

Identifying the Victims of Compliance Violations

If someone is robbed while walking in the street, then we can clearly see who the victim of the wrongdoing is. But some forms of corporate crime can appear to have no victims, or sometimes the identity of the victim is not clear. For example, who is the victim of insider trading? Is it the current shareholders? Are all shareholders harmed, or only those who would also have traded their shares if they too were in possession of the nonpublic information? What about other investors who are not shareholders but could have been if they had bought or sold had they had the same information? Whether or not we can identify the victims does not change whether wrongdoing has occurred.

Seeing the Victims of Bribery and Telling Their Story

In 2020, Debra Parris was living in a north Dallas suburb and working as a program manager at an Ohio-based adoption agency that facilitated international adoptions for U.S. families seeking to adopt children from Uganda, Poland, and elsewhere. Debra worked with Margaret Cole, who founded the agency in 1990. Debra's work also brought her into contact with Dorah Mirembe, a Ugandan citizen and resident who provided legal representation and adoption-related services to the agency. Between 2013 and 2016, Debra and Dorah were involved in adoptions of more than 30 Ugandan children by U.S. families, and the agency received more than $900,000 in adoption fees.

Adoption can be a wonderful way to bring children and adopting families together. In fact, one of my nephews is adopted. He spent the first few years of his life in an orphanage in India and is now a wonderful young man who is deeply loved and cherished by his adopted family here in the United States. While many international adoptions benefit children like my nephew, they are sometimes controversial, not only because adoptees are taken far away from their home country and any remaining family members, but also because of the large sums of money involved in the processing of such adoptions. Still, in my mind, Debra does not fit the profile of someone who I imagine would be involved in bribery and other criminal activity.

On August 17, 2020, the DOJ issued a press release titled "Three Individuals Charged with Arranging Adoptions from Uganda and Poland Through Bribery and Fraud." A thirteen-count indictment had been filed against the three of them, and Debra and Dorah were both charged with one count of conspiracy to violate the Foreign Corrupt Practices Act (FCPA), a U.S. federal law that provides that it is unlawful for any U.S. person or U.S. company to offer, pay, or promise to pay anything of value to any foreign (non-U.S.) government official for the purpose of obtaining or retaining business.

While Dorah remains at large at the time of this writing, Debra and Margaret have since pleaded guilty to some of the charges. Debra and Dorah (and others) had paid bribes to Ugandan government officials in order to facilitate the adoption of children who were not properly determined to be orphans, including children whose birth parents were still alive. Thankfully, these children were returned to their birth parents.

These were innocent children who were unlawfully taken from their families and home country and transported thousands of miles away because a group of adults engaged in bribery and other wrongdoing. As a parent myself, I cannot imagine the pain and suffering endured by the children, their birth families, or the families who innocently tried to adopt the children.

One can imagine that writing the press release must have been a very difficult task for whomever at the DOJ's Office of Public Affairs was tasked with writing it. The release describes the impact of the wrongdoing in a compassionate and human way and focuses on the human stories of those who were harmed. Some of the most hard-hitting quotes in the press release include the following:

> **"The defendants allegedly resorted to bribery and fraud to engage in an international criminal adoption scheme that took children from their home countries in Uganda and Poland without properly determining whether they were actually orphaned. The defendants sought to profit from their alleged criminal activity at the expense of families and vulnerable children."**
>
> - Acting Assistant Attorney General Brian C. Rabbitt of the Criminal Division

> **"As a result of this alleged conduct, prospective parents were deceived, hundreds of thousands of dollars were misused, and innocent children were displaced from their homes."**
>
> - U.S. Attorney Justin Herdman of the Northern District of Ohio

"These three defendants preyed on the emotions of parents, those wanting the best for their child, and those wishing to give what they thought was an orphaned child a family to love... Parents, prospective parents, and children were emotionally vested and were heartbroken when they learned of the selfishness and greed in which these three engaged."

- Eric B. Smith, Special Agent in Charge of the FBI's Cleveland Field Office

Bribery and corruption are far more than just the illegal actions of the bad actors. The wrongdoing of Debra Parris, Margaret Cole, Dorah Mirembe, and the many others involved or complicit in this wrongdoing brought significant harm to many children, their birth families, and the U.S. adoptive families. No doubt, this matter also likely had a very negative impact on the law enforcement officials and regulators who pursued justice for these innocent people. For those of us working in ethics and compliance, we can do more than simply write policies and train employees on antibribery laws. We should, of course, help employees understand what they can and cannot do to comply with these laws, but we can also help them see how complying with the law and policies helps protect other people. Often, the victims of bribery are amongst the most vulnerable people in society. We humanize our ethics and compliance programs when we see and value these people and their human stories.

When Employees Become Victims and Lose Their Livelihoods

Operation Car Wash (also known as Operação Lava Jato) was the name of a broad criminal investigation in Brazil in 2014 that involved a wide array of wrongdoing, including money laundering and bribery—including the case I referenced at the beginning of this chapter. The investigation involved various companies, including Petrobras (the Brazilian state-owned oil company) and Odebrecht (now known as Novonor), as well as hundreds of people who were arrested and convicted (including several prominent politicians in Brazil).

Odebrecht was fined a staggering $2.6 billion by the DOJ. All of this information was captured in the press and media, so I will not rehash what has been covered elsewhere and in much more detail.

A few years ago, I heard Olga Pontes, the then Chief Compliance Officer of Odebrecht, speak at a conference. Olga is highly respected in the ethics and compliance community, and she was hired by Odebrecht after the scandal had erupted (to be very clear, she was hired as part of the cleanup operation and was not part of the problem). Her speech and presentation at the conference I attended were impressive. Many would have viewed the task as daunting, but I remember Olga spoke calmly about the situation she stepped into and the impressive work she and her team did. She shared a slide that showed the number of employees Odebrecht had each year between 2006 and 2018. In 2013 (remember, Operation Car Wash was launched in 2014), Odebrecht employed approximately 182,000 employees. By 2018, Odebrecht employed approximately 48,000 employees. A staggering total of 134,000 positions were eliminated in the space of around five years (not taking into account that the number could have been more, as certain areas, including the compliance team, grew in headcount during that period). The wrongdoing resulted in 134,000 human beings losing their jobs at Odebrecht alone, and that figure does not even account for the impact felt by people who relied on those employees, including their families and other dependents.

Some of the newspapers did report on the human impact, but this coverage was minimal in comparison to the headlines about the fines, the wrongdoing, and those who engaged in the wrongdoing. In 2017, The Washington Post published an article by Marina Lopes and Nick Miroff titled "A corruption scandal wrecked Brazil's economy. Now, workers face the consequences." The article told the story of Ricardo Coelho, a former engineer at Odebrecht, and the impact the scandal had on him and his career. In writing about Ricardo's story, Lopes and Miroff described him as "once a top executive at the Brazilian construction giant Odebrecht" who "found himself stranded with no prospects." Ricardo eventually traded his 27-year career as an engineer and opened a hair removal salon.

Stories like this are useful when we seek to engage leaders, managers, and supervisors on ethics and compliance. Focusing on the human impact can help them see that compliance violations are about more than just fines and penalties. Employees can lose their jobs and incomes, and their career prospects are also often impacted by their association with the corporate wrongdoer. Ethics and compliance programs should not exist only to protect corporations and other organizations from risk and harm; they can—and must—help protect the organization's employees.

Regulators Show Signs of Seeing the People Who Need to Be Protected

While regulators and enforcement agencies are, understandably, often focused on the wrongdoing and the wrongdoers, there have been several important and recent speeches by key regulators highlighting the importance of seeing the human stories in ethics and compliance and the importance of helping people make the right decisions. Lisa O. Monaco, the U.S. Deputy Attorney General, delivered a speech in New York City on September 15, 2022, in which she said, "We will continue to engage and protect victims—workers, consumers, investors, and others." And in March 2023, then U.S. Assistant Attorney General Kenneth A. Polite delivered a speech in Miami, Florida, in which he spoke of "human suffering... in nearly every town across this country. Across this globe." Polite went on to talk about "the depth of our human capacity," how he sees his role and that of other prosecutors as "community problem-solvers," and the need for people to "step outside of our offices, our homes, embrace a broader sense of community, and engage our brothers and sisters on the challenges facing us all."

I think this demonstrates that regulators are not simply focused on whether or not laws have been violated; they are seeing and they aim to help the people and the communities the laws are meant to protect.

People-focused leaders and managers must do the same. I urge you to set high expectations for yourself and for your organization's leadership. These expectations should extend to employees and to the ethics and compliance program that protects them. As a leader, I want to ensure people go home physically and psychologically safe, knowing their financial and professional livelihood is not at risk because of ethics and compliance issues. A human-centric ethics and compliance program sees, values, and helps employees as people, and is critical for any employer who says that their employees are their greatest asset.

HUMANS AREN'T DATA POINTS

Actionable and measurable data can help monitor how your organization's ethics and compliance is doing, and it can also help measure whether initiatives and strategies are effective and working. While hotline data, for example, can be helpful for tracking and reporting to the Board and other stakeholders, it is important to not lose sight of the human stories and experiences behind those numbers. Our aim should be more than to "not lose sight of the human stories" and instead to see and hear them clearly.

By only looking at whether the data is in line with benchmarking averages, we will fail to see the people whose stories and experiences are behind that data (and the impact on those people). The numbers and data help to reveal whether you have an effective program to support and help your employees and other people, but don't forget that an effective program should serve, and see, the people it is meant to help and not just view them as statistics or data points.

ADAM BALFOUR

CHAPTER 5

THE SPEAKING-UP PROBLEM

We just talked about the humans directly impacted by wrongdoing—but what about the humans who became aware of or directly observed the wrongdoing and who did exactly what programs are designed to encourage them to do: to speak up? There is a real, measurable, and lasting impact on people who make the difficult decision to report wrongdoing. Humanizing the ethics and compliance function in your organization requires thoughtfully—and proactively—acknowledging this fact.

Unfortunately, the speak-up experience at many organizations tends to focus only on gathering facts and information to determine potential liability for the organization. The person speaking up may simply be seen as a source of information. Their human experience is treated as secondary, if it's considered at all.

Remember: A report concerning a single incident of inappropriate behavior may not seem significant to a large organization that has thousands of employees, but a single instance of harassment can have a devastating, lasting impact on the person being harassed. The incident is of great significance to the person who experienced the wrongdoing and who then took steps to report it. Speaking up is often a painful process, so it's critical that we normalize the process, make employees feel heard, protect them from retaliation, and reassure them that the issues they raised are being looked into and resolved in a timely manner.

Make the Most of the Moment

When someone speaks up, you have an immediate opportunity to build trust—or destroy it—depending on your process and on how the organization responds. A number of factors can quickly and permanently destroy trust in the speak-up process—as well as in the organization's values and its leadership—including a bad experience for the individual involved, a negative perception internally about the process, retaliation, and blacklisting. These can have an incredibly damaging impact, including on the individual's family, causing others to believe that speaking up is not safe. Trust can be maintained, however, if the person is treated with respect and care. That means not only looking for factual information that could help an organization manage liability, but also demonstrating empathy.

Speaking up is, and should be, something people feel compelled to do because doing so can have a positive impact, demonstrates their loyalty to the organization, and supports a desire to see organizational justice and fairness in the workplace. As many codes of conduct encourage, people who have relevant information should speak up, but simply making that statement will not build a habit or sustain a lasting culture of speaking up. The organization has to ensure that the act of speaking up leads to a positive outcome and is less painful than staying silent would be.

When we intentionally make the speak-up process more compassionate and humane, we help ensure that speaking up does not become a one-time or immediately regrettable decision. When someone has a bad experience speaking up or is retaliated against, often others will become aware, and that experience can have a chilling effect on them. "Secondhand" retaliation is often as damaging as "firsthand" retaliation.

And remember: Treating employees with respect and dignity is not at odds with managing potential liability for the organization. In fact, doing so will likely help reduce the risk of labor or other legal claims against the organization and can reduce the likelihood that someone will feel the need to escalate their concerns to regulators.

The Myth of "Creating" a Speak-Up Culture

I think too many organizations and E&C professionals talk about a "speak-up culture" as if it were the starting point: Get people to speak up somehow, and then create a speak-up culture based on that. I think that's backwards, and it places the burden on the individual. Speaking up is the outcome of company culture. When an organization demonstrates care for employees, it creates trust and psychological safety that can then make people more comfortable speaking up. Caring comes first. Human-centric organizations need to move beyond the idea of a "speak-up culture" and instead build a "culture of care" in which both the organization and the individual demonstrate shared responsibility for protecting each other's interests.

What's a Whistleblower Anyway?

The term "whistleblower" has developed a somewhat negative connotation over the last few years, reflecting the actions of those individuals rather than describing what they often are. They are, in most instances, people who care; they care for the organizations that employ them, they care for their fellow employees and those who may be harmed by wrongdoing, and they care about fairness and legal standards.

People like Cynthia Cooper, who spoke up about the wrongdoing at WorldCom and was featured with Sherron Watkins and Coleen Rowley as Time magazine's Persons of the Year in 2002, do not see themselves as heroes, but instead as people who were doing their jobs.[14]

While it is encouraging to see U.S. regulators providing ever-increasing financial rewards to individuals who have spoken up (including an October 2020 award by the U.S. Securities and Exchange Commission of "over $114 million to a whistleblower whose information and assistance led to the successful

---

[14] Time quotes Cynthia Cooper as saying "We don't feel like we are heroes," in "2002: The Whistleblowers," Time December 30, 2002 / January 6, 2003, https://time.com/5793757/the-whistleblowers-100-women-of-the-year/

enforcement of SEC and related actions"[15] which was more than doubled by the May 2023 award of "nearly $279 million, to a whistleblower whose information and assistance led to the successful enforcement of SEC and related actions"[16]), it's important to note that not all whistleblowers are likely to receive significant financial rewards, and these rewards can take years to pay out, during which time the individual may both have no income and be incurring legal fees. This person may endure years of extreme stress and uncertainty while waiting to learn whether there will be a payout at all. People can try to negotiate a contingency fee arrangement with any legal representation they obtain, but that is not always a certainty, and such arrangements may not cover legal fees associated with any counter claims filed by the organization.

Even with a remote possibility of a significant payout, I have not come across any evidence that indicates people who have spoken up are primarily motivated to do so for financial gain. A 2019 article in The Washington Post by Dana Gold[17] highlighted that whistleblowers are not motivated by the financial rewards, nor by taking potential issues directly to government regulators; instead, Dana Gold found that "the overwhelming majority of employees who see problems want to blow the whistle internally first" and that "in reality, most whistleblowers are motivated by a deep sense of loyalty to their employers and are exercising both a high degree of professional ethics and a belief that their employers will address the problem... Whistleblowers who report externally typically do so because the problem is significant and their employers have failed to address it or engaged in reprisal (or both)."

---

[15] "SEC Issues Largest Ever $114 Million Whistleblower Award," U.S. Securities and Exchange Commission, May 5, 2023.

[16] SEC Issues Record $114 Million Whistleblower Award," U.S. Securities and Exchange Commission, October 22, 2020.

[17] Dana Gold, "Five myths about whistleblowers," The Washington Post, April 5, 2019, https://www.washingtonpost.com/outlook/five-myths/five-myths-about-whistleblowers/2019/04/05/8a5de2ac-5624-11e9-814f-e2f46684196e_story.html

> " . . . in reality, most whistleblowers are motivated by a deep sense of loyalty to their employers and are exercising both a high degree of professional ethics and a belief that their employers will address the problem . . . "

HEARD ON THE HOTLINES

Many people don't know how many reports their organization receives through the hotline each year, nor what issues are most commonly raised. Maybe they imagine the hotline as a red telephone under a glass dome on the CEO's desk. If the red phone rings, there's a problem. If it's silent, all is well.

Most ethics hotlines are run by third parties that specialize in the intake of allegations of misconduct on behalf of organizations and allow people (employees or others) to make confidential or anonymous reports. Some organizations limit the types of matters that can be reported through the hotline, but most publicly promote the hotline and accept reports of anything deemed appropriate.

One may think the majority of matters raised through ethics hotlines involve criminal activity, fraud, theft, or significant wrongdoing, but the reality is quite different. It is estimated that around 65-70% of hotline reports relate to HR matters, including allegations of discrimination, harassment, conflicts of interest, workplace bullying, and retaliation.

Recognize Retaliation

Nothing chills a speak-up culture faster than retaliation (or even the perception of it). Organizations must take immediate steps to address the risk of retaliation when someone speaks up or participates in an internal investigation. A 2018 Ethics & Compliance Initiative (ECI) survey found that 72% of people who experience retaliation said it took place within three weeks of reporting their initial concerns. Organizations can minimize the risk and impact of retaliation by proactively assessing the risk of retaliation when someone speaks up or participates in an internal investigation, ensuring investigations are treated as a priority by investigators, and conducting post-investigation retaliation checks.

Nearly every organization that has a code of conduct includes a statement to the effect of "we have a zero-tolerance policy when it comes to retaliation," but the reality is very different for many people who have spoken up. Rates of reported retaliation are only getting worse. According to the NAVEX 2022 Hotline Incident Management Benchmark Report, "in 2021, reports of retaliation nearly doubled"[18] compared to 2020, and a March 2021 Global Business Ethics Survey Report found that "retaliation for reporting was at critically high rates across all countries in 2020". [19]

There are too many examples of people who have spoken up and "blown the whistle" on significant wrongdoing at organizations and then faced horrific consequences for doing so. Too often, people who have spoken up about wrongdoing were retaliated against and treated terribly when they should have been rewarded and treated with respect, not only for following their conscience, but also for following company policy.

These acts of retaliation can take many different forms. It is important to know what retaliation looks like so we can help stop it when it occurs.

One of the challenges with retaliation is that it can involve behaviors that, in other situations, might be appropriate—like changing someone's working hours or time off, moving someone to a different role, or changing their job responsibilities, or providing a negative performance review. But when retaliation drives such actions, the individual is unfairly harmed. This is one reason why, according to the NAVEX Benchmark Report mentioned above,

---

[18] "Risk & Compliance Hotline & Incident Management Benchmark Report," NAVEX, 2022.
[19] "The State of Ethics & Compliance in the Workplace: A Look at Global Trends," Ethics & Compliance Initiative, March 2021, https://www.ethics.org/global-business-ethics-survey/#non-member-download

allegations of retaliation are less likely to be confirmed as true by internal investigations ("24 percent [of claims about retaliation] were substantiated, well below the overall substantiation rate of 43 percent"). It can be very difficult to show motivation or other evidence of retaliation in those situations, as those under investigation can often provide plausible and believable explanations for their actions.

While far from exhaustive, the following list are examples of retaliatory acts:

- Negative feedback or other performance reviews that impact an individual's compensation, chances of promotion, or ability to keep their job. When someone has spoken up, it is important that their future performance reviews and other evaluations be carefully monitored to detect potential retaliation. Speaking up does not mean that someone should not receive appropriate feedback or constructive criticism about their job performance, but they should not be punished or negatively impacted because they spoke up.

- Reductions in compensation (including, for example, taking away overtime work) or otherwise changing their benefits.

- Transferring the employee to a different role or otherwise changing their responsibilities, including, for example, being reassigned away from desirable projects and given less desirable work or assigning a near impossible amount of work so the employee is set up to fail.

- Changing someone's hours or schedule, which can have a negative impact on an individual's personal life or other commitments.

- Verbal, physical, or psychological abuse, including bullying and gaslighting. An example of this was when Watergate whistleblower Martha Mitchell was "kidnapped, sedated, drugged." In speaking about Mitchell, Kate Clarke Lemay, a historian at Washington's Smithsonian

National Portrait Gallery, said "People denied that this happened to her. In today's phrase, they gaslit her, they called her crazy, they used that age-old reference for women as hysterical... She was the whistleblower and we respect her today." [20]

- Spreading rumors, attempting to disparage the individual's reputation at the organization, or otherwise harming their reputation to prevent the individual from being hired by another organization in the future (known as "blacklisting").

- Ostracizing the individual either by intentionally ignoring or treating them differently. According to the previously mentioned March 2021 Global Business Ethics Survey Report, this was the most common form of retaliation, reported by 25% of people globally who experienced retaliation. Workplace ostracization can involve excluding a person from work-related activities directly tied to their role (such as excluding them from meetings) or other more socially focused work-related activities (excluding the individual from team lunches or other work social events).

Retaliation can look subtle to bystanders, but the effects on a victim can be severe. If someone expresses concerns about retaliation, their concerns should be taken seriously and not quickly dismissed as trivial or belittled as insignificant. Not everyone who speaks up will suffer long-term career or financial harm as a result, but many do experience significant and sometimes lasting harm.

Here are a few examples of the human impact of retaliation on people who have spoken up:

- A November 2019 article in the Financial Times shared the story of "Mary," "a former Deloitte employee." Mary spoke up about a Deloitte partner who had sexually assaulted her, "kick-starting a process that led to her eventual redundancy." She shared: "Much worse than the

---

[20] David Smith, "'They called her crazy': Watergate whistleblower finally gets her due", *The Guardian*, April 2, 2022.

incident itself is the fact that the company I thought was going to protect me then betrayed me and protected him and hung me out to dry... That has been much more damaging in the long run."[21]

- The Office Of The Whistleblower Ombuds has a set of "Whistleblower Survival Tips" that includes guidance for potential whistleblowers to "consult your loved ones" before speaking up because doing so "can have long-lasting personal impacts for you and your loved ones. You could become blacklisted from your industry, subjected to public smear campaigns, and undergo severe psychological trauma."

- A 2021 study found that the income of whistleblowers can drop by 7.3-8.6%.[23]

- A 2012 article in Social Medicine[23] cited research published in 1990 that highlighted the consequences for whistleblowers. The findings were based on a study of 233 whistleblowers in the U.S. and found that 90% lost their jobs or were demoted, 27% faced lawsuits, 25% got into difficulties with alcohol, 17% lost their homes, 15% were divorced, 10% attempted suicide, and 8% went bankrupt. While this study is very dated, I am doubtful that a more updated study would reveal that the human impact of retaliation has diminished.

Stop Making Compliance Painful and Laborious

Imagine going to a police station to report something and after reporting the issue, the police officer tells you that you need to report your concern by calling 911 or 999. This hypothetical situation would be absurd and infuriating, right? Organizations need to make sure they aren't creating the same experience for

---

[21] Madison Marriage, "Betrayed by the Big Four: whistleblowers speak out," *Financial Times*, November 19, 2019.

[22] Aiyesha Dey, Jonas Heese, and Gerardo Perez Cavazos, "Cash-for-Information Whistleblower Programs: Effects on Whistleblowing and Consequences for Whistleblowers," SSRN, April 30, 2021, https://ssrn.com/abstract=3837308.

[23] Jean Lennane, "What Happens to Whistleblowers, and Why," *Social Medicine* 6, no. 4 (May 2012), https://www.bmartin.cc/dissent/documents/Lennane_what2.pdf.

their employees when people try to speak up. Are your employees speaking up through approved or encouraged reporting channels and then being told they need to report the same issue or concern to the organization's ethics hotline? If people experience the process of speaking up as being difficult or too burdensome, they may question if your organization wants them to speak up, or they may feel it is too much hassle to do so. Organizations should invest in making the speak-up process as simple as possible for the person speaking up and making sure employees don't have to report concerns through multiple channels before they are heard.

If the speak-up process is too painful or laborious (for example, if the hotline takes too long to report matters or lacks empathy, or if someone reports a matter to a manager and is then told to call the hotline), it will put people off from continuing the reporting process or they won't want to do it again. If finding guidance requires too many "clicks," then only the most motivated and persevering individuals are likely to find the guidance. If a policy or procedure is too long and filled with technical terminology, then it won't be read or understood—and possibly not complied with either. Doing the right thing should be made as easy as possible; if doing the right thing is emotionally and logistically hard to do, an organization should not be surprised when overworked people aren't doing what the organization hopes they will.

. . . And Close the Loop After Someone Has Spoken Up

Imagine watching a TV series or movie. You have invested time and energy and tried to guess how it will all end. Just as the end is nearing and you are about to find out what happened, a message appears, saying "this movie/TV show and the storyline were resolved to the satisfaction of the production team and are now considered complete. Thank you for watching." While this might have (definitely would have) been a better way for Game of Thrones to have ended, it would be largely unsatisfying for most other movies and TV shows, and it would make me less likely to watch a show or movie by the same producer/director in the future. No one wants to invest time watching and then not know how something ends. Yet, this is the experience so many people are left with when they have spoken up with concerns and are simply given the canned response, "your concern has been looked into and appropriate actions, if any were deemed necessary or appropriate, have been, or will be, taken by the organization." The person raises a concern, perhaps even helping the investigation by being interviewed and providing information. Then, nothing.

I get that there are totally valid reasons organizations don't provide completely transparent responses, but we need to find ways to respond that both recognize the reporter's humanity and assure the reporter that their story has been heard (even if the allegations or concerns raised are unfounded). Remember, when someone speaks up, it is a moment of trust. In that moment, trust can be destroyed or it can be rebuilt or sustained if the person is—and feels—listened to and respected. Even if you cannot share the complete ending of the story when it comes to the investigation, look for human ways to provide closure for the person who spoke up.

ADAM BALFOUR

CHAPTER 6

LEARNING AND LISTENING: HUMANIZING TRAINING AND EMBRACING FEEDBACK

In order to get organizations to be compliant and to act ethically, we need the people who work for those organizations (often including not only the organization's employees, but also temporary or contracted workers and people working on behalf of the organization) to do certain things or avoid certain behaviors. It is important, therefore, that we help people relevant to our organizations understand what they need to do in their specific roles. Sometimes this knowledge is fairly straightforward and common sense, but other times there is a legitimate need for additional communication or educational efforts. That's where formal training comes in.

Formal Training: Not Just a Formality

Regulators consider training important. The U.S. DOJ says, "[a]nother hallmark of a well-designed compliance program is appropriately tailored training and communication." Organizations engage in many types of formal training, including live training (often PowerPoint-based) on particular topics (the code of conduct, specific risk areas such as anti-bribery or antitrust laws, or specific requirements for regulated industries such as health care, pharmaceuticals, and finance), online training (which sometimes allows people to "test out" through an initial quiz at the start of the course, shortening the course and the final testing questions if it appears that the individual has a good base knowledge and understanding), and various other forms of communications about compliance, such as posters in the break rooms, TV displays, and emails.

In order to redesign and rebuild ethics and compliance for humans, I think we need to make what might appear to be a subtle, but important change: We need to leave behind the thinking about "Training and Communication" and instead move toward "Learning and Engagement."

The issue with "Training and Communication" is that we focus on the intent of the ethics and compliance programs rather than on the impact on the target audience. We have all sat through trainings that do not result in learning, and we have all received communications that are not engaging. I recall hearing a story several years ago in which a well-intentioned, experienced lawyer thought it would be a good idea to cover the legislative history of the Foreign Corrupt Practices Act of 1977. (unless Jeopardy! ever asks about the legislative history of the FCPA, it will have been a complete waste of time and effort.) A key mantra to keep in mind is that not all training results in learning, and not all learning will look like training.

Online training and PowerPoint-based trainings can—when done effectively and with the audience's learning objectives in mind—support learning; however, I have found there is more creative freedom in focusing on the learner outcome and not simply the traditional means of training. The adult learning theory provides that how adults learn is fundamentally different from how children learn. Malcolm S. Knowles, a well-known expert on adult learning, found that the adult learner experience can be leveraged as a way to help adults learn. Adults, unlike children, have life experiences to use as a framework, and we draw on those life experiences as a resource for learning and relating to new ideas and concepts. We can help employees learn about ethics and compliance in the following three ways in particular:

1. Telling Stories
2. Movies, TV Shows, and Other Pop Culture
3. Learning Through Experience and Coaching

#1. TELLING STORIES.

Stories can be powerful and effective for engaging employees in the moment, as well as helping to make the content memorable. In a blog post for Harvard Business Publishing's Corporate Learning, Vanessa Boris wrote: "Organizational psychologist Peg Neuhauser found that learning which stems from a well-told story is remembered more accurately, and for far longer, than learning derived from facts and figures. Similarly, psychologist Jerome Bruner's research suggest[s] that facts are 20 times more likely to be remembered if they're part of a story."[24]

There are many types of stories your organization can use, including: (1) relevant headlines about other organizations; (2) stories of wrongdoing that has occurred in the organization in the past, and how the organization addressed the issue(s); and (3) stories that show how speaking up helped the person who spoke up, and how the organization listened to them and demonstrated care. These types of stories can have a powerful impact not only to encourage adherence to standards and make the standards more understandable through real-life examples, but also to show that other people have spoken up and to normalize the speak-up process. Scrubbing these stories to remove the identities of those involved can help protect against retaliation and avoid further embarrassment or shame for those involved (unless your organization intentionally wants to "name and shame" employees). Scrubbed stories can have a positive impact on helping people learn and can help reinforce organizational standards.

Stories can be effective in helping adults learn about ethics and compliance in real-life terms; however, we have to ensure that the stories are relevant, relatable, and will have the desired impact. I used to think that ethics and compliance stories from the headlines were the most effective way of helping people learn, but many people struggle to connect with the story of a C-suite wrongdoer they have never met who has been fined millions of dollars (an amount most of us will

---

[24] Vanessa Boris, "What Makes Storytelling So Effective for Learning?," Harvard Business Publishing, December 20, 2017, https://www.harvardbusiness.org/what-makes-storytelling-so-effective-for-learning/.

never come close to having). Stories from within an organization can have a much greater impact since they are more relevant and relatable, but don't assume that all employees will be impacted the same way (even if the story seems like it should have an impact).

CHILDREN'S STORIES CAN OFFER (OCCASIONALLY DARK) LESSONS

In Beatrix Potter's "Peter Rabbit," Peter's mother tells him and his siblings not to go steal or eat vegetables from Mr. McGregor's garden because Peter's "father had an accident there, he was put in a pie by Mrs. McGregor." (By "accident," she means murdered and eaten). This story was effective in deterring Peter's siblings, but it did not work for Peter. Perhaps the rewards outweighed the risks for him, or perhaps the story wasn't told in a way that resonated.

Stories can be effective in helping adults learn about ethics and compliance, but we have to ensure that the stories must be relevant and relatable to have the desired impact. I used to think that stories from the headlines were the most effective way of helping people learn, but many people struggle to connect with a C-suite wrongdoer they have never met who has been fined millions of dollars (an amount most of us will never come close to having). Stories from within an organization can have greater impact. But don't assume that all employees will be impacted the same way (even if the story seems like it should have an impact). There will be Peters in every organization, and we need to find ways and stories to connect and engage with them.

#2. MOVIES, TV SHOWS, AND OTHER POP CULTURE.

Well-known movies and television shows can provide inspiration for a range of ethics and compliance lessons. For instance, from:

- **Frasier:** Dr. Frasier Crane's line, "This is Dr. Frasier Crane. I'm listening." This can be a reminder for leaders, managers, supervisors, and investigators that it is not simply about employees speaking up, but the importance of ensuring the organization listens to people who speak up and that they feel heard.

- **Parks and Recreation:** Most workplace comedy shows have a host of workplace romantic relationships and other conflicts of interest, as well as other wrongdoing. Parks and Recreation, for example, involved bribery of a government official (when Leslie and Ben tried to bribe a government official at Li'l Sebastian's memorial concert to keep their relationship secret), employees having side businesses that involve a conflict and/or abuse of their position (Tom Haverford's Entertainment 720 company caused a conflict with his government job and was told by Chris Traeger, "you emailed everyone at City Hall and told them to come to a club that you own to buy alcohol that you invented. Government employees can't use their power to enhance their personal wealth"), and a large number of romantic relationships involving the main characters that often spilled into workplace romances (I counted twenty-one relationships involving the ten main characters.)

- **Ted Lasso:** This show offers ample messages on how caring leaders can deliver results, how pressure can impact individuals (such as Nate), and how having trusted colleagues (whether Dr. Sharon or the Diamond Dogs) can help with isolated decision-making.

- **Jurassic Park:** The series can be used to highlight the need for risk assessments when entering new markets or innovation, the risks of bribery and of disclosing confidential information, and the need to learn from past mistakes and avoid repeating the same mistake multiple times (theme parks and velociraptors just do not seem to be a good combination, no matter how many times one tries the concept.

- **Star Wars:** Did the Jedi leaders put too much pressure on Anakin? Obi-Wan said to Anakin, "You were the chosen one! It was said that you would destroy the Sith, not join them! Bring balance to the Force, not leave it in darkness!"[25] That is a lot of pressure for anyone to deal with, and those are high expectations to live up to!

(See the Additional Resources section for additional ethics and compliance discussion questions inspired by the Star Wars movies.)

#3. LEARNING THROUGH EKPERIENCE AND COACHING.

Through decades of research, the Center for Creative Leadership has developed a "70-20-10 framework" for learning. [26] Their framework provides that our learning occurs through the following ways and ratios: "70% challenging experiences and assignments," "20% developmental relationships," and "10% coursework and training." While online trainings can provide a variety of data points and other metrics (which seem to be of particular interest to organizations pursuing ESG rating agency recognitions), it is a mistake in my opinion if we focus only on the 10% of learning that provides the most quantitative data and forget that the main objective is to help the relevant learners learn what is most relevant for their role. When we ensure that ethics and integrity are intentionally and regularly part of the employee experience (70% learning) and leverage the influence leaders, managers, and supervisors

---

[26] Lucas, George, dir. *Star Wars: Episode III- Revenge of the Sith*. 20th Century Fox, 2005. 2 hr, 20 min.
[26] "The 70-20-10 Rule for Leadership Development," Center for Creative Leadership, April 24, 2022, https://www.ccl.org/articles/leading-effectively-articles/70-20-10-rule/

can have in coaching employees and ensuring standards and values are lived up to (20%), we can more fully tap into the myriad ways in which adult humans learn. The impact of focusing on this 90%, and not only the "10% coursework and training" of traditional online and PowerPoint trainings, can be measured through organizational culture surveys, tracking whether leaders are talking about ethics and compliance, and asking if employees have heard from leaders on these topics. You can easily get data by running a monthly contest in which employees are eligible to win a small prize if they indicate if their leader or manager talked about the Compliance Tip of the Month generated by the ethics and compliance team or similar initiatives involving diversity, equity, and inclusion. Impact is also reflected in the volume and types of matters raised through the various speak-up channels, including anonymity and substantiation rates.

Both quantitative and qualitative data can indicate whether employees are learning, what that learning is, and whether the ethics and compliance program is well designed, adequately resourced, and working in practice.

The Value of Asking for Feedback

As we know, a post-training survey can give you a glimpse of the effectiveness of your training. Surveys are also a useful tool to gauge (and improve upon) the success of your program as a whole.

Ethics and compliance programs do not exist in isolation; they are directly impacted by the organizational culture, the pressures people face, how these people operate, the tone from leaders and managers in their part of the organization, other programs and policies, and a host of other factors. While the program framework should be led by the ethics and compliance team, the perceptions, experiences, ideas, and feedback of other employees are absolutely critical and relevant to determining the success and effectiveness of the program in practice.

Some of the best ideas I have heard recently to improve our ethics and compliance program came from people who are not part of our core compliance team (though they come up with awesome ideas, too). People in other functions see things differently, and they are the people who are more likely facing some of the risks and challenges the program is trying to help with. Seeking out conversations, feedback, and ideas from colleagues in different parts of your organization will both help improve your program and help you understand what is going on in the different parts of the organization your program is meant to support. It is hard to say you have a well-designed program that works in practice if you don't seek out feedback and input from different stakeholders and viewpoints in the organization.

Employee surveys are a relatively easy way to gather employees' insights, input, and experiences. Surveys can be conducted in various ways, including through online surveys (which can go to a larger audience, but provide less opportunity for dialogue) and through individual or group feedback sessions (which can lead to deeper and more wide-ranging conversations, but generally include a smaller number of employees and take longer to conduct than a two-minute survey). There are benefits in whatever survey format you decide to use and, ideally, feedback is solicited and received through various formats to ensure employees at all levels and locations have the opportunity to provide their thoughts.

One concept I have yet to fully develop and deploy is an "Innovation in Integrity Award." The idea would be to allow employees from across the organization to submit their ideas for how the ethics and compliance program could be made more effective, what would be the challenges or obstacles to putting their idea into practice, and how their idea would add value to the ethics and compliance program and the organization as a whole. Incentivizing employees to share their ideas—either with a cash prize, trophy, or other recognition—is likely to generate good ideas that the ethics and compliance team can implement, ensure that employees know their role as it relates to ethics and compliance,

❝ *Incentivizing employees to share their ideas—either with a cash prize, trophy, or other recognition—is likely to generate good ideas that the ethics and compliance team can implement, ensure that employees know their role as it relates to ethics and compliance, and ensure that ideas are heard and valued by the organization.* **❞**

and ensure that ideas are heard and valued by the organization.

You won't necessarily act on all employee feedback and ideas received—nor will most feedback and ideas radically change the ethics and compliance program design and how it operates—but nevertheless, feedback should be obtained from employees. We should not only rely on employee voices in terms of the speak-up process, but also look to engage employee voices, perspectives, and feedback in a variety of proactive ways. If you do act on feedback or an idea provided by an employee, make sure to follow up with the person to let them know that their idea was still appreciated and considered even if there were reasons their idea was not acted on.

Seeing and Hearing 2.0

When we talk about ethics and compliance, we are essentially talking about the human experience—that of the different people we are trying to encourage and incentivize to act in certain ways, and that of those who would otherwise be harmed by the acts or omissions of others. Thus, we have a responsibility to ensure our ethics and compliance programs are closely aligned with efforts to support and advance diversity, equity, and inclusion. Together, we can celebrate and support diversity within our organizations and our communities and advance the human experience for all humans. This is another reason why seeking input from others is so important. When people are sharing their stories with those of us who work in ethics and compliance, it is on us to ensure those human stories are told and shared.

There are various other ways we can support the diversity of our workplace, including being thoughtful about the visuals and pictures we include in our written policies and training materials. As a regular PowerPoint user, I am amazed that people other than white males are significantly underrepresented when you search for pictures involving professional jobs. Type in "CEO" and all 50 of the first 50 pictures with people in them are male (at least this was the case the last time I conducted this search). Presentations become part of the story being told in your organization, so make sure you consciously think about whose story is being told (and whose story is not being told) by the pictures and images you include in trainings and communications.

You can also embrace the diversity of your organization by communicating with people in their preferred language and making sure that people with visual or hearing challenges are included (one of Bridgestone's 2023 videos to support the Compliance Tip Of The Month was a recording by someone who communicated in sign language and included subtitles for those of us who cannot understand sign language).

Learning can come in many forms (e.g., feedback conversation with manager, individual or group training, informal discussion about the scenario, etc.), and helping people learn from ethical and compliance shortcomings can support an organization's culture, further a growth mindset, and reinforce the importance and expectations around an organization's standards.

Are Your Investigations Intentional?

When we are intentional about focusing on human stories and experiences in our ethics and compliance programs, it can also change how we look at certain pillars of our programs. An example of this is internal investigations. Far too often, internal investigations make speaking up a painful experience that becomes an immediately regrettable one-time action.

If your organization only conducts internal investigations to protect and mitigate legal and reputation harm, then you need to think more broadly about how and when they're employed. Internal investigations are also a way of showing your employees that the organization actually, genuinely cares and listens when people speak up; demonstrating a commitment to protect and promote your organization's standards, values, and culture; helping to identify policies or procedures that are unclear, nonsensical, or in need of updating; and revealing other areas for training and learning.

This means internal investigations should not only ask questions about facts and data, but also ensure that the person who is speaking up is heard and feels heard. That means demonstrating genuine empathy and care for someone and genuinely listening to their emotions and their perceptions. It doesn't mean you must agree with the story presented, but you must patiently and respectfully listen. Seeing investigations only as "liability mitigation" is narrow-minded and unnecessary.

And, speaking of investigations, be mindful about your timeframe. Some internal investigations will take longer than others due to factors such as complexity, number of people to be interviewed, materials to be reviewed, and specificity of the allegations. Many companies consider 30 days as the target within which to complete most investigations. From an organization's standpoint—and perhaps the investigator's, too, if their workload is high—30 days is not a lot of time. However, from the perspective of the person who reported actual or alleged wrongdoing, or that of the person suffering the wrongdoing, 30 days can seem like a really long time.

If someone is dealing with harassment, retaliation, or workplace bullying, then 30 days will feel a lot longer to the individual than it will to the organization, especially if there is not much communication from the organization about what is happening. As is shown in NAVEX's latest benchmarking report, the reality is that 22% of organizations had a median case closure time of 100 days or more.

Investigations should never be rushed. They must be made a priority to ensure that wrongdoing is addressed in a timely manner and to ensure that employees are, and feel, seen and valued. Speaking up is often hard; it doesn't need to be made worse by the organization taking what might feel like an eternity to respond.

EVEN ETHICAL LAPSES CAN BE LEARNING OPPORTUNITIES

Ethical lapses and other noncompliance issues in an organization can present learning opportunities for those involved, as well as other employees and the organization as a whole. However, "learning opportunities" are simply opportunities for learning; learning does not automatically occur, and not helping the relevant employees learn from the situation is a missed opportunity. If an ethical lapse has occurred in your organization that presents a learning opportunity, it is important to (1) understand who the learning opportunity is for, (2) identify what the potential learning is, and (3) develop, and then implement, a learning plan that actually supports—and results in— the desired learning.

CHAPTER 7

LOOK WHO'S TALKING: LEVERAGING THE VOICE OF LEADERS, MANAGERS, AND SUPERVISORS

I am currently teaching one of my daughters how to ride her bike. After taking four hours of e-learning and certifying that she has read and understood the policy, "how to safely ride your bike," I am confident she should now know how to ride her bike. To ensure her ongoing engagement and commitment, she also signed an acknowledgment that she understands that violating our cycling rules may result in disciplinary action, up to and including no TV for a week. She is super excited about cycling.

Okay, while I am actually helping my daughter learn to ride her bike, we did none of the above. I'm not a cycling instructor and have no experience teaching a kid to ride a bike, but I am taking my best shot at it, and my less-than-perfect teaching is more effective than putting her in front of a screen and thinking she would learn that way.

In the same way, **managers and supervisors don't need to be ethics and compliance experts to help their teams and to have a positive impact on the culture of ethics and compliance.** Having managers and supervisors regularly talk about ethics and compliance (even if the message isn't perfect) makes a positive, lasting impact. A less-than-perfect message from an employee's direct manager (which can be based on an outline or talking points that the E&C team provide) is much more effective, personal, and likely to resonate with employees than staring at a computer screen or certifying about policies. E-learnings, policies, and certifications can play a valuable role in your program, but they cannot replace the role of managers and supervisors.

Just Ask

Over the years, I've been asked by a few people from other organizations "how do you get the CEO and other senior leaders to talk about ethics and compliance?" The answer is simple: You start by asking the C-suite to talk about ethics and compliance. Yup, it is that simple. Your CEO and other senior leaders are incredibly busy, but I have yet to come across a senior leader who is driven to deliver results and leads with integrity and who has not immediately said "yes"to helping reinforce organizational values and using their voice for good.

Regulators expect "tone at the top" and—more importantly, in my opinion—I think most employees want to hear directly from their organization's leaders about what they really think. This is an opportunity for senior leaders to reinforce the key messages of the ethics and compliance program and also to share their personal stories about their careers, any ethical dilemmas they have faced, how and when they spoke up, and what their experience was like in doing so. People connect with people, and they connect with human stories. Your organization's senior leadership are hugely influential people who will inevitably have interesting and impactful stories to tell. If you haven't asked your senior leaders to talk about ethics and compliance, then reach out to them today and find opportunities that work for their schedules to make it happen.

Check Your Ego

Many people, including myself, have experienced the workplace frustration of saying something that is challenged or dismissed, yet later hearing the same words go unchallenged, acted on, and even praised when said by someone more senior.

As frustrating as this experience can be, it is a reminder that communication (and your ability to influence others) depends not only on the wording of the message, but on who is communicating that message and how they do so. When we focus on what we want the impact of a communication to be, we can then devise a plan for the most effective way to achieve the desired intent, as well as to whom and how such messages will be communicated.

TONE AT THE TOP

There is no single metric that can tell you whether an ethics and compliance program is effective, but the closest indicator may be whether leadership regularly talks about the importance of ethics and compliance in ways that are relevant and resonate with their employees. But don't just take my word for it. The DOJ's "Evaluation of Corporate Compliance Programs" (updated March 2023) highlights the importance of "top leaders" who "set the tone for the rest of the company" and how "middle management" has "reinforced those standards" through "words and actions," "encouraged or discouraged compliance," and "modeled proper behavior to subordinates."

Furthermore, Deloitte in 2014 described tone at the top as the "first ingredient in a world-class ethics and compliance program." The message must start at the top and must be amplified, cascaded, and tailored by managers and supervisors throughout the organization to reach every employee. If this isn't taking place, then integrity is not a top priority and the organization will face challenges ahead.

The ethics and compliance function must have a credible, respected voice that is listened to and able to influence others in the organization. An appropriately staffed ethics and compliance team will have the experience and knowledge to speak and communicate on many topics. This team is often best suited to speak on specialized areas such as antitrust, corruption and bribery, and how to conduct investigations. But **while the ethics and compliance team should be regularly seen and heard by employees, they cannot be the only ones using their voices and communicating with employees about ethics and compliance.**

Just as many companies rely on spokespeople and other endorsements to help influence consumer behaviors and decisions, an effective ethics and compliance program also needs similarly influential people to use their voices and authority to engage employees and influence their behavior and decisions.

Leaders, managers, and supervisors have powerful, persuasive voices that can help engage employees. A 2018 paper by the Ethics & Compliance Initiative found that "managers and supervisors set the tone by talking about ethics" and that "employees who agree that their managers and supervisors talk about the importance of ethics are almost 12x more likely to believe that their organization encourages them to speak up."

Similarly, a January 2020 report by Ethisphere also found that "employees whose managers frequently discuss ethics and compliance topics with them … are 2X more likely to be comfortable approaching their manager with concerns or questions," "90 percent more likely to have faith in their manager's commitment to non-retaliation," and are "24 percent more likely to believe they have a personal responsibility for making sure the company does the right thing."

Leadership must set the tone through their own behavior and by what they tolerate in behaviors of others, but they also must set the tone through their words, because they have voices that are listened to and influential in the organization. Bear in mind, however: Employees can tell when an executive is

" Employees can tell when an executive is being sincere, both from their words and when their words are inconsistent with their actions. They can also tell when the executive is scripted, so make sure to choose leaders who will be genuine, confident in openly talking about ethics and compliance, and who have credibility with employees when it comes to talking about integrity. "

being sincere, both from their words and when their words are inconsistent with their actions. They can also tell when the executive is scripted, so make sure to choose leaders who will be genuine, confident in openly talking about ethics and compliance, and who have credibility with employees when it comes to talking about integrity.

5 Tactics for Success

There are a variety of ways to engage leaders, managers, and supervisors and encourage them to use their voices to support ethics and compliance, including:

1. **Being Visible and Vocal:** This can mean having leaders present at all-hands employee meetings or town halls, or creating special events where senior leaders, including the C-Suite and even theBoard of Directors, can talk openly and address questions from employees. A panel of senior leaders discussing ethics and compliance with a large group of employees can make a significant impact and demonstrate whether and how much integrity matters to your organization. These types of events can be powerful, especially if the panelists are willing to open up and share about matters including:

    - ethical dilemmas they have faced in their careers;
    - examples of when they have spoken up (and what happened as a result);
    - the importance of leaders, managers, and supervisors in supporting ethics and compliance;
    - how ethics and integrity tie in with strategic initiatives and other organizational priorities; and
    - examples of times employees did not achieve the expected standards of ethics and integrity (and what happened as a result).

2. **Involving Leaders, Managers, and Supervisors in Trainings:** I am not suggesting that you ask the leaders and managers in your organization to conduct trainings on high-risk issues or complex topics such as antitrust and antibribery; however, they can co-present on topics such as the importance of speaking up, how to speak up, and the role of managers and supervisors in supporting a culture of integrity and inclusion. Even if a leader or manager is not comfortable or suited to co-presenting the contents of a training, they can use their voice to introduce the topic and explain why it is important.

3. **Sharing a "Compliance Tip of the Month":** Some organizations create a short compliance tip of the month that is usually the equivalent of a single slide and provides some high-level information on a particular topic (gifts and entertainment, promoting respect and dignity, the importance of DEI, assessing candidates for integrity, password-sharing, third-party risk management, new policies, etc.). These tips are usually fairly quick and easy to put together, and they often require little or no preparation on the part of a leader or manager to incorporate and speak about them in a team meeting. While the content of these tips is relevant, I think the real value of this tactic is that leaders, managers, and supervisors are the ones delivering the message.

4. **Being an Active Listener:** As I have mentioned several times in this book, speaking up can be challenging. Leaders, managers, and supervisors can make it easier and psychologically safer for employees to speak up by not passively waiting for people to speak up, but instead proactively, regularly asking employees if they have any concerns, are facing any ethical issues, and are aware of any wrongdoing. Even if an employee does not have anything to raise or report at that moment, regularly asking employees and showing care can signal that speaking up is safe, normal, and encouraged, and that the manager or supervisor wants to be a speak-up channel for the employee.

5. **Walking the Halls:** In his book, *The Accidental Compliance Professional,* Roy Snell describes a "people-first approach" he has taken to "spend time with people" since "most compliance problems are caused by people." Snell goes on to say, "part of the reason why the compliance profession was created and why many have failed at it is because leadership and compliance were not spending enough time with the people causing the problems. More importantly, leadership and compliance were not spending enough time with the people who knew where the problems were."

Conversations about ethics and compliance should not only take place in meeting rooms or windowless conference rooms where training occurs; it is important for employees to feel that leaders have a genuine interest in what they do and where they work, and that they make the time and effort to meet them there. Leaders (and the ethics and compliance team) must get out of their offices (and be provided with the travel budget to do so) and go spend time with employees in person. This allows for more human interactions between senior leaders and employees, enables leaders to understand the challenges employees face, and demonstrates that leadership is accessible and cares. Senior leaders can use these "walk the halls" conversations to ask employees about what they do, talk about the importance of organizational values, and understand how employees perceive and experience the organizational culture.

Senior leaders have many demands for their time and must be intentional about investing time in connecting with employees. A 2022 Harvard Business Review article by former Medtronic CEO Bill George recommended that CEOs aim to spend 30% of their work time (the amount of time that George did as Medtronic CEO) with front-line and lower-level employees. In contrast to George's approach, Michael Porter and Nitin Nohria reported in a 2018 Harvard Business Review article that CEOs in their study "spent 72% of their total work time in meetings" and only "about 6%" of their time "with rank-and-file employees." Connecting with employees is an important part of a leader's responsibilities and should be given priority in the schedule.

While walking the halls can be challenging in remote workforces, hybrid workforces, and global organizations, leaders, managers, and supervisors need to find ways to proactively and regularly connect with employees on ethics and compliance. Walking the halls might come naturally to some leaders, but others might need to allot time to go connect with employees, schedule coffee breaks (in person or virtual), and travel to remote teams, allowing time to connect with employees outside of meetings.

Listening: The Role of Roundtables

It is amazing what people will share with you and how it will make them feel if you sit down over a cup of coffee and ask them for their thoughts. Ethics and compliance teams can bring people together in this way by setting up small roundtable discussions for employees and one or more leaders to sit down and openly talk about ethics and compliance in the organization.

The purpose of small roundtable or group discussions is to create an opportunity and a safe space for leaders to connect with employees (especially if the leader does not regularly work with the employees in the roundtable) and to facilitate an open conversation in which the leader can ask and be asked questions. Keeping the group size to no more than eight or ten people can allow for a more intimate and comfortable setting, giving employees the chance to talk about matters or ask the leader questions that they might not feel comfortable asking in a large town hall meeting.

I like to encourage leaders to start these conversations by sharing some examples of how they have faced and addressed ethical challenges in their career and asking some open-ended questions that will allow employees to take the conversation in different directions. I have sat through many ethics and compliance roundtables, and I am always amazed by the engagement and openness of these conversations once employees feel it is safe to talk and open up. I find these small group conversations can help create dialogue and build trust between leaders and employees and also provide leaders a chance to hear the real challenges and pressures employees face on a daily basis.

Setting up ethics and compliance-focused roundtables can take some work and coordination. You need to find leaders (with time on their busy schedules) who will be effective at leading a conversation on ethics and compliance and who will be open to questions and feedback from employees. You also need to find willing employees who will volunteer or otherwise agree to participate in these conversations.

I find these roundtables are most effective when they take place in person and in a comfortable setting that will support openness and conversation (e.g., not a conference room with a large table that creates distance between the participants, but instead, a more social area that has comfortable chairs and, ideally, coffee).

Today's technology does allow these roundtables to be conducted virtually, but I have found that virtual sessions only work well when people use their cameras so they can see each other. In these formats, the leader running the roundtable also needs to be more intentional about making sure that each of the participants has an opportunity to speak.

These types of roundtables are useful for building a speak-up culture. Many organizations talk about wanting or having a speak-up culture when what they mean is that they want and expect employees to speak up. Human-centric organizations recognize that a speak-up culture does not start with employees speaking up. Instead, employees speaking up is an indicator of an effective speak-up culture. An effective speak-up culture is focused on ensuring that leaders, managers, and supervisors are using their voice to speak up on ethics and compliance and that they are building trust and communicating well with employees. When leaders invest their time in sitting down with employees, talking about their experiences, and listening to employees, they help to build and sustain a culture that will support employees speaking up.

CHAPTER 8

SOMETIMES COMPLIANCE IS AWKWARD

One of my favorite coffee mugs reads "Awkward is my specialty." It seems appropriate for any compliance officer (or HR professional) to have, since compliance can often be awkward. Policies don't exist in isolation; they live alongside the pressures and social norms that your employees live in. Compliance programs cannot shy away from taking a stance on issues where needed, but an effective, employee-centric program will anticipate and help people with the challenges and awkwardness that might result from complying with your policy. Seeing the awkwardness in situations and offering ways to help employees through the awkwardness will go a long way to help your employees and advance the credibility and effectiveness of your program.

Leadership speaker and author David Cottrell has said, "doing the right thing isn't always easy—in fact, sometimes it's real hard—but just remember that doing the right thing is always right."

It is easy to write policies that say "you must never..." or "it is never acceptable to...." But remember: Written policies do not exist in isolation; they are influenced by pressure, isolated decision-making, the behavior of others, organizational culture, and what is permitted and promoted within the organization.

Often, organizations need to take a strong stance on certain areas, such as antitrust, antibribery, and sexual harassment. That is entirely fine and appropriate. But we must recognize that complying with some standards is easier said than done, and we must examine the pressures an employee might face in trying to comply with the standard or deciding whether or not it is in their interest to comply.

Employees can find themselves in awkward situations, especially when a standard set by their organization is perhaps different from that of other organizations. For example, organizations have different standards when it comes to gifts, meals, and entertainment. Some companies do not tolerate any giving or receiving, some companies allow infrequent and modest giving and receiving (what constitutes infrequent and modest is also subjective to each organization), and others have generous policies that allow for what some would consider to be lavish or extravagant giving, but with restrictions on the offering or giving of items of value (directly or indirectly) to government or union officials.

A vendor or supplier might, with good intentions, want to give your employee a gift or take them to an event that is in violation of your policy but that does not violate the vendor or supplier's policy. If your organization has a more restrictive policy than that of another company, your employees could find themselves on the receiving end of a generous gift or offer and having to decide between running afoul of your policy or potentially damaging an important business relationship. If your employee has an appropriate relationship with the vendor or supplier, your policy puts that employee in an awkward position—they are going to have to decline the offer or return the gift, and that can be socially awkward.

It is not helpful to write a strict policy that says "no" and does not lean into the challenging situations that employees might find themselves in.

That is the awkwardness of ethics and compliance programs in action. We have two options: Option one, to leave the employee alone with the policy and see how they do (neither recommended, nor useful for the employee or the E&C program); option two, to acknowledge the potential awkwardness and lean in to help the employee in dealing with it (recommended, with a much higher chance

66 *People, for better or worse, connect with and are influenced by people more so than by policies.* 99

even if no individuals are speaking up.) It is hard to speak up, and it can often be awkward, so we need to recognize that and find ways to search for signals and signs of ongoing issues. That is the awkwardness of ethics and compliance programs in action. We have two options: Option one, to leave the employee alone with the policy and see how they do (neither recommended, nor useful for the employee or the E&C program); option two, to acknowledge the potential awkwardness and lean in to help the employee in dealing with it (recommended, with a much higher chance of actual compliance).

Helping them does not mean that a policy waiver will be granted or a blind eye turned to help avoid the awkwardness. Rather, it can involve walking the employee through the matter and helping them prepare for a potentially difficult conversation. This could be in the form of helping draft an email message that says "thank you very much for your thoughtful gesture. While I very much appreciate the kind offer, please understand that I am unable to accept it because of our organization's policies. I hope you understand that this is not a personal rejection of generosity, but that I must comply with my organization's policies." This type of message will not work in every situation, and it does not mean that the sender or recipient of the message will necessarily be happy, but it does serve to help with the awkwardness that compliance can sometimes involve. I have personally used this message on several occasions (mainly to test how it works in practice), and I do not believe my relationships with any current or potential vendors have been harmed by my transparency.

Ethics and compliance can also feel awkward when there is extreme pressure to achieve certain targets, perhaps even with incentives on the line, and when many others (including people you know and trust) are complying with the pressure in the organization. The right thing to do in this situation is to stand up and blow the whistle, but that can seem like an incredibly daunting prospect. Someone in that position might (understandably) draw one of the following conclusions:

- *"Maybe this is fine, or at least not as bad as I think it is, because other people are doing it."*

- *"This is bad and wrong, but why should I speak up if others are not?"*

- *"I don't want to speak up against my colleagues and my boss. I don't want to get them into trouble, and I think there will only be negative consequences if I speak up."*

- *"I don't think anyone will believe me, and nothing will be done."*

There are so many examples, including the examples of Wells Fargo and Ernst & Young mentioned earlier in this book, where individuals have either actively gone along with the majority or simply remained silent as a bystander.

People, for better or worse, connect with and are influenced by people more so than by policies. While we should hope and continue to expect that individuals will speak up, an effective ethics and compliance program for humans has to recognize how pressure can impact and silence individuals and that there is a need for real and actual governance. The Board of Directors should have an understanding of the actual organizational culture—not simply what the Human Resources department and the organization says is the culture. There must also be proactive reviews of business practices and results by those functions known as the second and third lines of defense, as well as by external and intendent advisors, such as independent Board members, independent auditors, and third parties.

The second and third lines of defense—typically consisting of the HR, legal, ethics and compliance, safety, and risk in the second line and internal audit in the third line—should also proactively and regularly ask employees about pressures and determine whether there are signals that issues are occurring even if no individuals are speaking up. It is hard to speak up, and it can often be awkward, so we need to recognize that and find ways to search for signals and signs of ongoing issues.

Effective ethics and compliance programs for humans cannot be built and run solely from one's office or desk at headquarters. We need to see and experience the locations where other employees work to grasp the everyday pressures, influences, and challenges they face; to determine whether compliance with a stated standard is achievable; and to understand what additional support measures may be needed to ensure compliance.

ADAM BALFOUR

CHAPTER 9

WHAT'S IN IT FOR ME?
THE ROLE OF RECOGNITION AND INCENTIVES

In many organizations, the ethics and compliance program is seen as the department that stops the fun or otherwise gets people into trouble. Sometimes that is true; we aim to stop inappropriate behavior and ensure consequences for those who commit wrongdoing. There should be consequences based on how people act and whether they perform to expectations, and those consequences can either be negative (disciplinary measures) or positive (incentives, rewards, and other recognitions). Regulators also see the need for incentives and disciplinary measures, as can be seen from the U.S. Department of Justice's "Evaluation of Corporate Compliance Programs" (updated March 2023)

- "Another hallmark of effective implementation of a compliance program is the establishment of incentives for compliance and disincentives for non-compliance";

- "some companies have also found Compensation structures that clearly and effectively impose financial penalties for misconduct can deter risky behavior and foster a culture of compliance. At the same time, providing positive incentives—personnel, such as promotions, rewards, and bonuses for improving and developing a compliance program or demonstrating ethical leadership—have driven, can drive compliance."

In 2022, a speech by Deputy Attorney General Lisa O. Monaco reiterated the importance of reflecting ethics and compliance in "compensation systems," including on the "deterrence side" and the "incentive side." While the Deputy Attorney General's comments on employing "clawback provisions" (where pay or other compensation would be "clawed back" by the organization from individuals who are involved in any misconduct) has generated a lot of questions on how such arrangements can work in practice (particularly in countries other than the U.S., where labor laws mean that such arrangements are not permitted and/or near impossible to enforce), her guidance and observations are worth reading.

Some traditional ways to recognize and incentivize people include promotions, bonuses, and advancement into management or leadership roles. When determining the balance between "carrot" and "stick" incentives, the organizational culture has to be considered, as does which specific incentives are most appropriate for the organization, and which will actually be used in practice. For some organizational cultures, greater focus on positive incentives might be more aligned with how the organization engages employees and drives certain behaviors. If such an organization were to introduce more punitive measures, such measures could be perceived by employees as unfair or harsh, even if such measures are used by other organizations, and there could be a reluctance by management to enforce such punitive policies.

In contrast, some organizational cultures may be more influenced by punitive measures and those measures effectively used to achieve compliance. In such organizations, celebrating individuals with awards for integrity may not be as effective as at other organizations.

The above are simply two rather polar opposite examples. There are many ways positive incentives and negative consequences can be effectively introduced to ensure that ethics and compliance are achieved in practice. Whatever approach your organization decides to take, the approach should be intentional, designed with the culture in mind, and followed in practice to achieve the desired result.

Monaco captured this point well in a September 2022 speech discussing the balance of incentives and punitive measures when she said, "as everyone here knows, it all comes back to corporate culture." Corporate or organizational culture is a key factor and must be considered when designing systems to encourage compliant and ethical behaviors.

Following are examples of ways to effectively incentivize and recognize people who have demonstrated ethical and compliant behaviors. I have intentionally stayed away from some of the more obvious, traditional incentive and punitive measures, since those examples can be found elsewhere. While the use of incentives is a much-talked about topic of late, Joe Murphy, a visionary in this field who is rightfully known by many as the "Godfather of Compliance," wrote an incredibly comprehensive paper back in 2011 called "Using Incentives in Your Compliance and Ethics Program."[27] If you are looking for additional ideas on how to successfully include incentives in your ethics and compliance program, I would I highly recommend reading Joe's paper, as well as Uri Gneezy's book, Mixed Signals: How Incentives Really Work.[28]

Leading with Integrity Awards

As we know, leaders, managers, and supervisors are a key element in achieving a culture of ethics and compliance throughout the entire organization. Many take their responsibilities very seriously and should be recognized for their contributions. One way to help recognize leaders' contributions is to create an award program called the "Leading with Integrity Awards" and allow employees to nominate leaders with a brief note on what the individual does to help create and sustain a culture of integrity.

You will receive nominations for individuals who are well-known for their support of the ethics and compliance program, but **there also may be some surprises, as**

[27] Joseph E. Murphy, "Using Incentives in Your Compliance and Ethics Program," Society of Corporate Compliance and Ethics, November 2011, https://assets.hcca-info.org/Portals/0/PDFs/Resources/library/814_0_IncentivesCEProgram-Murphy.pdf

[28] Uri Gneezy, Mixed Signals: How Incentives Really Work, Yale University Press, 2023.

you are likely to be made aware of people who are strong advocates for ethics and compliance but whom you and your team had little or no knowledge of.

This is a concept we launched during my tenure leading Bridgestone's ethics and compliance program, and it is perhaps one of my favorite initiatives we developed. The nomination process is fairly simple, asking for information such as the name of the nominee and the reason why he or she is being nominated. This information can be collected through an online survey tool or even by email. After receiving the nominations, we created a panel of senior leaders to select the winners. We then had the CEO and other senior leaders announce the names of the winners on an ethics and compliance leadership panel that was attended by several hundred other employees.

Whether or not you have the budget to award a cash prize or a trophy, it can make a real impact on the winners and the rest of the employees if the CEO calls out one or more employees by name, sharing what they did and their impact.[29]

Annual Performance Goals

Many organizations continue to use annual performance assessments that are tied to the individual's performance objectives for a particular year. Ethics and compliance truly are everyone's responsibility, but the responsibility each individual has is different relative to their role; therefore, each individual's objectives and measurements should be somewhat tailored.

Effective goal-setting and priority alignment can help ensure ethics and compliance are considered as the organization pursues strategic priorities, as well as that efforts to support and advance ethics and compliance are recognized and rewarded. Compliance shortcomings or even a lack of effort to support ethics and compliance can also be reflected in an individual's feedback, compensation, and overall performance evaluation.

---

[29] For more information about how to launch a similar award program, please see Adam Balfour, "Recognize (and grow!) compliance and ethics leadership in your organization," *CEP Magazine*, February 2021, https://compliancecosmos.org/recognize-and-grow-compliance-and-ethics-leadership-your-organization.

Annual performance goals tied to ethics and compliance can be particularly useful for engaging leadership at all levels. Leaders, managers, and supervisors should consider realistic and challenging objectives that will be assessed throughout the year. The maturity of your program should also be considered in developing performance goals tied to ethics and compliance, as this will help ensure that employee objectives are both reflective of where the program currently is and aligned with the direction the program is headed.[30]

Below are some examples of ethics and compliance-related goals, some of which may work for your organization.

GOAL 1: "I WILL TALK WITH EMPLOYEES AT LEAST ONCE A ____ ABOUT THE IMPORTANCE OF COMPLIANCE, ETHICS, AND INTEGRITY AND HOW THEY ARE RELEVANT TO THEIR ROLES." This goal is particularly relevant for leaders, managers, and supervisors, given how impactful it is when an employee's direct supervisor talks about compliance. One way to support leaders, managers, and supervisors in regularly talking about ethics and compliance is to develop a Compliance Tip of the Month, as discussed earlier in Chapter 7.

GOAL 2: "AT LEAST ONCE A ____, I WILL MAKE SURE TO ASK MY DIRECT REPORTS IF THEY HAVE ANY CONCERNS OR KNOW OF ANY WRONGDOING." While speaking up is always the right thing to do, it does not mean it is necessarily easy. As we've discussed, there are many reasons individuals may find it challenging to speak up. Speaking up can be an emotionally difficult experience for people, even if they are treated with respect and are not subjected to retaliation. We need to see, recognize, and validate this human experience. We can also help employees by placing more focus on the organization "listening" to people who have concerns to raise, and we can do that not only by demonstrating empathy and care when people speak up, but also by proactively reaching out to people and

---

[30] For more examples of annual performance goals, particularly for those in leadership and management roles, please see Chapter 7 "Does Your Organization Pursue A Culture Of Compliance And Ethics Through Annual Performance Goals?" The Compliance & Ethics Blog, January 27, 2021, https://www.complianceandethics.org/does-your-organization-pursue-a-culture-of-compliance-and-ethics-through-annual-performance-goals/.

initiating the conversation. This goal can be expanded to include indirect reports as well, if the leader has a sizable team and regularly conducts "skip level" meetings. Proactively asking employees about compliance issues or concerns can help address issues early on and reinforces that speaking up is encouraged and safe.

GOAL 3: "I WILL SPEAK ON AT LEAST ____ INTERNAL LEADERSHIP DISCUSSION PANEL EVENT(S) FOR EMPLOYEES DURING THE YEAR RELATED TO COMPLIANCE, ETHICS, AND INTEGRITY." As described in Chapter 7, there are a variety of ways in which your organization can engage leaders and leverage the power and influence of their voices. One such example we discussed earlier is to get leaders—especially members of the C-Suite—involved in leadership panels for large groups of employees. Getting leaders involved in trainings and panel discussions can reinforce the importance of the topic and make it relevant for and resonate with the target audience.

GOAL 4: "I WILL ENSURE 100% OF EMPLOYEES ON MY TEAM HAVE COMPLETED ANY REQUIRED ETHICS AND COMPLIANCE TRAINING (INCLUDING MEETING THE EXPECTED LEARNING OUTCOMES) OR ANNUAL DISCLOSURE CERTIFICATIONS BY THE DUE DATES." This goal also helps ensure that leaders, managers, and supervisors are accountable for the ongoing training and learning of the employees who report to them, as well as ensuring the timely completion of any other required items. Too many ethics and compliance teams spend too much time chasing individual employees to complete required actions; we can and should make leaders and managers responsible for ensuring that their teams are doing what is expected.

GOAL 5: "I WILL ENCOURAGE (OR REQUIRE) LEADERS AND MANAGERS TO SET THE EXAMPLE BY COMPLETING ANY ONLINE TRAINING REQUIREMENTS WITHIN 10 DAYS, RATHER THAN 30 DAYS." If a senior executive can carve time out of their busy schedule to complete a 30-minute online training, then so can other employees. Completing a compliance-related online training before the deadline can send a clear message about the need to prioritize compliance. It can also encourage what the DOJ refers to as, "demonstrated rigorous adherence by example." It can be helpful for leaders and managers to include a goal both that recognizes and reinforces how they "set the tone for the rest of the company" and that encourages them to model desired behaviors.

Leverage Other Existing Internal Incentive Programs

A number of organizations—particularly mid-sized and large organizations—use point-based reward systems that allow employees to recognize others through internal social recognition and "points" that can be redeemed for merchandise or other items of value. I have found that these systems can be effective to help directly and indirectly incentivize certain behaviors.

Watching short video messages from leaders on ethics and compliance.

During Bridgestone's an Ethics and Compliance Week that I ran, we created a series of short video messages from leaders on ethics and compliance and then asked people to complete a brief quiz and gave the person with the highest score a number of points. This encouraged people to watch the videos, and the short quiz helped to reinforce some of the points covered in the videos.

Encouraging Managers to Talk About Ethics and Compliance.

Ethics and compliance professionals often seek to directly influence and incentivize people to act in a certain way. This can be effective, but we can also incentivize behaviors indirectly. One example: Create a monthly contest in which employees can win points when their manager or another leader in their group talks about the Compliance Tip Of The Month (discussed in Chapter 7). This approach can be useful in several ways, not only because ethics and compliance will be discussed regularly, but also because it can reveal which parts of the organization are using the tips (and which parts of the organization need more encouragement and attention).

Make it Fun and Engaging

Ethics and compliance are incredibly serious, and we should respect their seriousness. However, simply because a topic is serious does not mean that we always have to approach the topic in a serious way. We can make serious topics fun and engaging. Of course, there are limits to this; some topics lend themselves to this approach more so than others, and we need to be careful that attempts to make something fun and engaging do not come across as childish or treat employees like children. In full transparency, I cringe when I see organizations that create childlike ethics and compliance scavenger hunts.

Gamification has been discussed by ethics and compliance professionals for several years; some have been more successful at "gamifying" E&C programs than others. During my tenure leading Bridgestone's ethics and compliance program, we successfully gamified aspects of its ethics and compliance program, including by creating the "Bridgestone Compliance Battle Royale" ("Battle Royale" for short). We first launched the Battle Royale back in 2019 as a way to engage our employees and make ethics and compliance feel more relevant and resonate with employees. We realized that if we created an effective marketing campaign and provided an engaging experience, we could change how people see and feel about ethics and compliance.

The Battle Royale started as a sixteen-team bracket event that took place over four days, but we have also run an eight-team bracket over three days. We divided different departments and parts of the business into teams and assigned them "team colors" to encourage a team spirit (some teams wore their team colors, and some created virtual backgrounds that showed their team colors). The contest is a daily elimination-style, head-to-head series of quizzes with between five and seven multiple-choice questions. We used an online tool to award points based on correct answers and the speed in which answers are given (you will soon realize that some of your colleagues are incredibly competitive). Since some teams were bigger than others, we determined the winner of each round (which we referred to as a "battle") based on the top five scores from each team. We ran the Battle Royale as an in-person event in 2019, but we found it also worked well as a virtual event during the pandemic, as people from other locations were also able to participate. We told people that ahead of time that much of the question content would be tied to our Compliance Tips of the Month, further motivating discussion about the Compliance Tips with their teams and driving traffic to our internal Ethics and Compliance intranet page, where the Tips (and other resources) were available.

SAMPLE BATTLE ROYALE QUESTIONS

- **Micro-trainings:** We included questions designed to reinforce expected standards and behaviors and to train employees on certain aspects of a new policy or expected behavior. "What should you do in this situation?" questions can reveal if people know what they should do and if existing policies and other guidance resonates with employees (though the competitive pressure of the competition may lead to some incorrect answers due to participants' desire to maximize their score for each question.

- **Education:** We included questions that referenced ethics and compliance-related headlines, as well as questions about the code of conduct and other policies.

- **Transparency:** We included questions relating to data about our ethics helpline, including the number of matters raised through the ethics helpline, the types of allegations raised, and the different features of our ethics helpline (you can speak with a live operator or submit information online, you can report anonymously, and you can communicate in your preferred language). As you might expect, we did not share confidential information about any particular ethics helpline reports, but we felt this was an effective way to transparently share information about our processes and the types of matters people seek help on and to demonstrate that others use the ethics helpline.

- **Promoting the Ethics and Compliance Program Agenda:** There were some questions employees were unlikely to know the answer to, but we were able to use the Battle Royale questions as a way to highlight new initiatives being launched and to explain the "why" behind those initiatives. There were also a number of questions based on our Compliance Tips of the Month, and this was another opportunity to encourage people to use the tips in future team meetings and conversations.

- **Identifying Communication Blockages:** While I generally favor making information about ethics and compliance available to as big an audience as possible, I have also found that limited distributions of information to targeted audiences can also be useful. For example, a quarterly email with ethics and compliance highlights can be sent to leaders and managers with encouragement that they, in turn, share with their teams. We included questions that were based on this information to understand in which parts of the organization this information was flowing freely and where we needed to spend a little more time and energy. In explaining the answer, we told employees where this information came from and encouraged them to reach out to their leader or manager to ask for the information too.

- **Retesting:** We also found benefit in including questions that re-tested questions and topics that people answered incorrectly in online training courses. This can be a good way to determine if the training and other communications are helping people to learn or if further efforts are needed.

Marketing Campaign and Leadership Engagement

Since the Battle Royale was a new initiative and designed to change how people saw and experienced ethics and compliance, we created a marketing campaign in the months leading up to the event that focused primarily on leadership engagement. We created an intentionally provocative tagline of "Compliance Isn't About Peace And Love—It Is About Winning A War!" and other teasers such as "16 Teams Will Battle—Only One Will Be Crowned The Champion" to generate buzz and interest. We also created a series of frequently asked questions to explain what the event was, when it would take place, what the teams were, and how it would work. We used an online bracket generator to seed the team; there was no rhyme or reason to the seed rankings the first year of the Battle Royale, but it provided some pressure on the top-seeded teams and stirred the underdog mentality in the lower-seeded teams.

Championship Trophy and Daily Recognitions:

As well as recognizing the winning team with a trophy engraved with the winning team's name (and reused each year), the individual who has the highest score of each day, regardless of their team's performance, is also recognized via email and awarded points through the employee points reward system that can be redeemed for merchandise or other items. What started as a one-time pilot event was met with standing room only conference rooms of people celebrating and cheering, as well as an expectation that it would—and since has—become an annual tradition for the last several years.

CHAPTER 10

POLICIES FOR HUMANS THAT HUMANS WON'T HATE[31]

Remember your first day at your job? Chances are, rather than worrying about meeting any of your new company's important goals for the year, you mostly were worried about how to log into your new computer and how to get your email to work. You probably wondered where the restrooms were, where to find good coffee, and maybe a few other critical pieces of information to help transition into your new role, or at least not mess it up on day one. With that in mind, here's what should not be on the agenda for brand-new employees: endless PowerPoint presentations with information that isn't relevant to the day one experience and won't be remembered past day three. There are so many more ways to introduce new employees to your ethics and compliance program—later.

As we discussed in Chapter 1, most people who get a new car do not immediately open and read the car manual in its entirety before driving the car for the first time. Yet this is how many organizations approach the new hire experience; we throw a number of policies at people, expect them to read them in their entirety, and then further overwhelm them with hours and hours of training. If new hire training does not result in long-term (or even short-term) learning, then what is the training actually doing and achieving?

---

[31] A note on this chapter: "Policies for Humans That Humans Won't Hate" is the title of a talk Lisa Fine and I have given on several occasions, and many of the ideas covered in this chapter are aligned with the content Lisa and I developed. Lisa is a rare and exceptional talent in the world of ethics and compliance. Not only is she an extremely talented lawyer and compliance professional, but she and the prodigious Mary Shirley founded Great Women In Compliance podcast (which Lisa and Lloydette Bai-Marrow are now leading into GWIC's next phase) and authored *Sending the Elevator Back Down: What We've Learned From Great Women in Compliance* (CCI Press, 2020). While credit is due to Lisa for many of the great, practical tips in this chapter, any and all errors (of which there are hopefully none) are solely my responsibility.

Time for a reality check. This chapter is called *"Policies for Humans That Humans Won't Hate."* It is not called *"Policies for Humans That Humans Will Love,"* and the reason for that is simple. No normal human being is ever going to love your ethics and compliance policies. You can make your policies colorful, fun-looking, and filled with 3D images, but no one is ever going to love them (if employees say they do, you either have sarcastic colleagues like me, or you should question their sanity). However, we can do a lot to make policies that humans won't hate – and will actually find useful.

Remember that Policies Cannot Replace Common Sense

In an April 2017 interview with ABC News' Rebecca Jarvis, former United Airlines CEO Oscar Munoz was interviewed about the forced removal of four passengers from United Airlines Flight 3411, including the assault of Dr. David Dao that resulted in him being knocked unconscious and dragged by the arms along the floor of the airplane in front of other passengers. When pressed on the root cause of the issue, Munoz seemed to criticize the policies relating to "the use of law enforcement aboard an aircraft." Munoz told Rebecca Jarvis, "we have not provided our front-line supervisors and managers and individuals with the proper tools, policies, procedures that allow them to use their common sense. They all have an incredible amount of common sense, and this issue could have been solved by that."

While I remain skeptical about the responses Munoz provided in his interview with ABC News, especially since United's response to the issue was so badly handled at the time (including comments that Oscar Munoz made in an email to United employees in which he wrongly described Dr. Dao as having acted in a "disruptive and belligerent" manner when the airline was "re-accommodating the customers"), I do agree that policies should not replace common sense or prevent people from using it. But to achieve actual compliance in practice, we need policies that are designed for humans along with a culture that encourages people to speak up when the policies are unclear. In other words, not only are human-centric policies built on common sense, they support employees when they demonstrate common sense.

If we approach policies as a substitute for common sense, the policies will end up as overly lengthy documents that try, but inevitably fail, to address every potential situation someone might encounter. And in fact, that approach tends to feel condescending or suggests to employees that the company believes they lack the ability to think for themselves. A prescriptive approach will neither predict every possible situation someone could realistically face, nor will it be engaging.

POLICIES DON'T MEAN A LACK OF LOWER HALF CLOTHING IS OKAY.

Ethics and compliance (and other) policies should be clear and practical for employees, especially if there is a risk that someone could lose their job or face other disciplinary action for violating an organization's policy. However, policies should also exist alongside common sense; if someone does something that any normal, reasonable human being would consider wrong or inappropriate, then the defense of "the policy doesn't specifically cover or prohibit that" is not a valid excuse. If human beings can figure out that "shirt and shoes required" policies don't mean a lack of clothing on one's lower half is okay, then organizational policies should focus on providing guidance that adds value, not aiming to cover every type of behavior that no normal, reasonable human being would need guidance on.

Start with "Why"

I like to go for a longer run on Saturday mornings around one of my favorite parks here in Nashville. As I finished one of my runs, I passed a small strip of what appeared to be a sidewalk with signs facing both directions and even signage on the ground that reads, "not a sidewalk."[32] With that many signs, it is rather clear that someone does not want this area used as a sidewalk; however, it really is not clear why they do not want it used as a sidewalk (especially since it is by a road), and I happily run on it when a car comes by.

When you create a policy or standard, you can get higher levels of compliance if you can explain the "why" behind it. If you cannot explain why you need a policy or standard, then you need to give some real thought to whether it is needed and set expectations low for actual compliance. More policies and standards is not always the answer. Provide people with clear guidance and help them understand why they should or should not do a particular thing.

But be careful here. While many policies exist, at least in part, because of regulator expectations or other legal requirements, I urge caution on making that the sole justification for why a policy exists. Recall our discussion in Chapter 3 about laws relating to parents and other caregivers of children. Our aspirations as parents and caregivers (and the reason why we care for children in the way we do) is not simply to meet the minimum legal standards.

There's always a bigger "why." Here's another example: While various antibribery laws are relevant to a policy on antibribery and anticorruption, an organization can frame the need for such a policy in more human terms. Perhaps, "Bribery and corruption of government officials often has a disproportionate impact on some of the poorest and most vulnerable people in society who depend on government actions to support their welfare and well-being. Our organization does not allow bribery and corruption, not only because they are illegal and immoral, but because doing so goes against our organizational values and

---

[32] If you are interested in seeing a picture of the sidewalk that is "not a sidewalk," please visit https://www.corporatecomplianceinsights.com/adam-balfour-ethics-and-compliance-for-humans/ for my December 4, 2022 #SundayMorningComplianceTip on "When Policies And Standards Make No Sense."

organizational purpose of helping our communities."

Highly regulated industries such as health care, pharmaceuticals, and banking are required to have a variety of policies, standards, and controls. Some may feel it is unnecessary—or, perhaps, unnecessarily difficult—to find and tell the human stories associated with policies explicitly required by regulators. Even in those situations, it is still possible to trace the standards back to a human story. Health care standards do not exist for no reason; they are intended to help protect the well-being of patients and other humans.

There's another danger to making rules and regulations serve as the sole "why" behind your policies. Doing so inadvertently sends a message to employees that the organization does not care deeply about a particular topic or suggests the policy would not otherwise exist if there were no laws in place and thus no risk of enforcement actions. That's why providing a human-centric reason behind a policy helps people understand why they should care about it. It also guides their actions and their decision-making, including around reaching out to someone else for guidance in the event that the policy is unclear or does not address the specific situation the employee is facing. Remember common sense? This is how you encourage it.

Who Does a Policy Need to Apply to?

Some policies, such as an organization's code of conduct, will apply to all employees; others will have a less global scope and be more specific to either a particular location or business unit (due to the nature of the operations at that location or business unit or due to local laws). Others still will be relevant only for certain roles; for example, your organization's internal investigations policy, to the extent one exists, is only relevant for those employees who conduct internal investigations. It is important from the outset to determine to whom the policy should apply so that the policy is drafted to be understandable, relevant, and resonate with that audience. Having a clearly defined target audience for a policy also helps to identify who in the organization plays a role in achieving the purpose the policy was designed to support.

After identifying the target audience, don't forget to tailor and fine-tune the policy. Make sure it's offered in the right languages and takes local customs into account, for example. The target audience might be in a location or business unit that will require a local policy to give further effect to the policy or some kind of learning opportunity to help reinforce it.

Socialize Draft Policies and Ask for Feedback

It does not take an experienced ethics and compliance professional long to draft a policy, but I know of few experienced ethics and compliance professionals who would create and roll out a policy in a short time frame. There are sometimes exceptions to this, but generally speaking, crafting good policies takes time.

When we focus on creating policies for humans, we want to make sure that the policies will actually work and be useful for those humans. Invest time in speaking with a variety of employees and other stakeholders who can provide relevant, valuable perspectives. This can be a time-consuming effort (I once conducted twenty socialization sessions over several months for one particular policy), but you will likely get useful, informed feedback and uncover gaps or opportunities for improvement for the initial draft policy.

This process also helps employees feel like they have a say in the standards that are applied to them. Additionally, it can assist with any change management required to successfully roll out the policy. You do not need to conduct twenty socialization sessions for every policy you launch, but think about which perspectives will help your policy be most effective, and spend the time to get it right.

Write for Humans in Human-Friendly Terms

Imagine sitting down with a novel and the first five pages are simply defined terms that explain who the characters are and other information about the story.

For example, *"Joe Bloggs: A pleasant and affable individual who everybody likes, right up until the end of the story, when you will find out he is the killer."*

Stories and novels do not begin that way, and, in most instances, apart from defining yourself by your name, this is not how humans tend to interact with each other.

Nothing says "overly lawyered" more than a policy that begins with a list of definitions and reads like a dictionary. Most employees will not flip back and forth from the policy page they are on to the defined terms. Using plain language can alleviate, or at least minimize, the need to use defined terms.

There are, of course, instances when defined terms can serve a useful purpose. It is very common for written contracts and other legally binding documents to contain a large number of defined terms. Specificity and precision matter, and defined terms can provide a way for parties to state their intentions, avoid potential issues or litigation, and argue when issues arise. Defined terms have a place, but they are not the only way to provide clarity and specificity on a topic; this is especially so when we are looking to communicate with people who are not lawyers.

Socializing draft policies with different stakeholders has yet another benefit: It can help the policy writer determine if using plain and simple language or a defined term will be most effective. If a defined term is considered appropriate and in common use, then the defined term should be one that a non-lawyer human being can readily and quickly understand. A definition term that reads *"The term 'foreign official' has the meaning as set forth in the Foreign Corrupt Practices Act of 1977, as amended, 15 U.S.C. §§ 78dd-1, et seq."* is of no value to anyone.

Don't Dump Everything into One Big Policy

Imagine getting on an airplane and, as you sit down next to a stranger (who inevitably has a crying child on their lap—I am often that stranger—or claims the armrest, and then some of your space), the safety briefing begins. Instead of the usual two- or three-minute safety briefing, the flight attendant tells you and the other passengers everything the pilot and airline crew need to know to operate the plane and what to do in the event of an emergency, including how to land a plane on the Hudson River like Captain Sully. Pilots, airline crew, and passengers all need to know what to do in the event of an emergency, but what they need to know varies significantly and is based on their specific role (recall that passengers sitting in the emergency exit row get an additional briefing).

Ethics and compliance policies must also reflect that different people in the organization have different roles; what is applicable and relevant to one employee might be very different from what another employee needs to know on the same topic. The lawyers of your organization need to have a detailed understanding of the applicable laws and regulations, but most employees in most organizations do not need to know the same information about the laws as the organization's lawyers. It is important to consider (as will be discussed in more detail later in this chapter) whether a single policy is appropriate and either flag in those policies which sections apply to which employees or break the policy down into different documents for different audiences.

Policies Can't Just Be About What NOT to Do

When it comes to areas such as antibribery and antitrust, there are a lot of things employees and organizations cannot do. It is important to provide guidance on these "no go" topics and danger areas, but we also cannot forget that there are many things employees can do (it is not illegal to take a customer for a cup of coffee, and it is not illegal to use information about your competitors that is in the public domain, for instance). Too many policies only focus on the things that people cannot do; the risk with this approach is that it leaves individuals, who have targets to meet and pressure to meet those targets, to their own devices to determine what they actually can do.

Policies should offer useful, practical guidance that helps employees navigate through what they can do, what they can't, what might be okay in certain circumstances, and when and to whom, they should reach out for guidance on. If policy writers put themselves in the shoes of the people to whom the policy will apply and also socialize the draft policy with stakeholders and the target audience, they can identify whether the policy will actually be useful and serve its purpose or if it leaves employees with too many unanswered questions.

Include Frequently (and Actually) Asked Questions

A well-written policy that can be conceptually understood by readers may still require some thought when it comes to putting the policy into practice in a way that aligns with the policy writers' intent. As discussed, stories can be a powerful and effective way to engage employees and help them learn and retain information. Policies can include realistic and real-life FAQs—ideally those posed during the socialization stage or at any other time. These FAQs are essentially mini-stories and can bring policy principles to life and help employees understand whether their intended actions are allowed and whether they should seek additional guidance.

I will sometimes aim for approximately half of policy content to be FAQs. Not only are FAQs helpful when rolling out a new policy, they can also be regularly updated to reflect new situations employees may face and expanded to include new questions.

How Many Ethics and Compliance Policies Should You Have?

Don't make the mistake of assuming that "if some policies are good, more must be better." I recently read about a traffic experiment conducted in Drachten, the Netherlands, in which the town removed the majority of the traffic lights and signs to improve road safety for drivers, cyclists, and pedestrians, with the thinking being that drivers were more aware of their surroundings, including other people, when required to think and not just rely on signs. The number of accidents decreased as a result.

Policies can be useful in the right culture when they provide appropriate guidance without employees abandoning other judgment and thought processes, but writing policies (or adding more of them) is not always the right option to achieve the desired outcome. So, how many policies should your organization have? The answer will depend not only on what risks your organization faces, but also the culture of your organization and an assessment of whether more or fewer policies will get to the desired outcome.

One Policy Might Not Be the Right Approach

Seek a balance between having a large number of policies and having policies that are so broad and that they feel more like an encyclopedia (both of which can be daunting and overwhelming for employees).

For some topics, one policy will likely suffice. For example, it is unlikely you will need multiple antiretaliation policies. However, topics such as antitrust can vary by applicable laws; also, antitrust laws are incredibly broad. Not all aspects of antitrust law are relevant to every department in the same way or need to be covered in a single policy; colleagues in the Human Resources department need to know about HR aspects of antitrust laws (for example, "no poach" agreements and wage-fixing). This is very different from what employees involved in trade associations or Sales and Marketing need to know (for example, how to gather competitive intelligence and develop pricing strategies). A single antitrust policy might not be as helpful or user friendly when compared with shorter, standalone policies and guidance on various antitrust topics. Having a good understanding of the risks your organization faces and who in the organization can help mitigate, amplify, or manage those risks can also help you determine how to approach policies and whether one policy on a particular topic is the right approach for your organization and employees.

Assume That Not Everyone Will Read the Entire Policy

By this point in the book, I expect you have no doubt gone back and read your

> **❝** *If I cannot explain the key points in four bullet points or fewer, then I will reconsider whether the topic is too complicated to cover in one policy and should be addressed differently.* **❞**

car manual in its entirety and would be willing to confirm through a "check the box" certification that you have "read and understood your car manual in its entirety." If you have still not read your car manual in its entirety by this point, then I feel reassured that you remain a human being.

As much as we want people to read policies in their entirety (and even ask them to certify as much), we should not assume that everyone will do so. If we lean into this assumption and accept it is likely reflective of reality, we can still find ways to engage and inform our employees about the policy.

In the United States, very lengthy documents are filed with the SEC when companies are offering to sell shares or other securities to the public. You can find these documents online. You may notice there is a "Summary" section near the front of the offering document (often referred to as "the box" since there is a rectangular box surrounding the text on each page of the Summary), which is intended to summarize the lengthy document in key terms. Earlier in my career, I served as a securities attorney in New York; in that time, I learned that few investors—who were often investing millions of dollars—read the entire offering document, but instead focused their time and attention on "the box." I apply a similar concept to ethics and compliance policies, assuming that employees can reasonably be expected to read a short summary of the key policy requirements. I generally aim to succinctly convey approximately 80% of the key aspects of the policy in four bullet points or fewer. If I cannot explain the key points in four bullet points or fewer, then I will reconsider whether the topic is too complicated to cover in one policy and should be addressed differently.

A Policy Is a Tool, Not a Purpose By Itself

Policies should not exist simply for the sake of having a policy on a topic; instead, policies should be tools to educate employees on a particular topic. When organizations create and launch new products, the product launch is supported by marketing and communication campaigns that initially raise awareness and then focus on making the product relevant and resonate with the target audience. There are many ways to help employees learn and understand; policies can serve that function, but we can also provide various learning and engagement opportunities that address relevant aspects of the policy for a particular audience. While some early communications are used to make employees aware of the policy, we should also leverage the concepts of brand relevance and resonance that we covered in Chapter 1 to connect with our target audiences and speak to them in ways that are relevant and will resonate with them.

Make Policies Easy to Find and Access

Companies do not create and launch new products with marketing and communication campaigns and then make their products difficult for potential customers to find; they want people to see and engage with their products and to build a successful future for the product. We also do not want to be like Luke Skywalker (Chapter 6 and Resource #2), hiding the Jedi Scrolls in a uneti tree on the planet of Ahch-To; policies must be easy for people to find and placed where someone could reasonably assume to find them.

As we discussed earlier, not all policies apply to all employees or have the same audiences, so you should take into account the audience(s) for a particular policy when determining where to make a policy accessible to employees. Some policies can be made available to the world at large (for example, your code of conduct), while other policies might only focus on a small number of employees or even be written procedures that most organizations would not want to share publicly. Here are some suggestions for how to make your policies available and accessible to the target audiences:

1. **Website:** A number of organizations make some of their policies available online. I find this can be useful for employees since it makes finding a policy easy and does not require anyone to log in to a secure IT environment to do so. Also, navigating policies online (particularly if you can search for terms) can help employees connect with the

relevant section and find the relevant guidance in a faster and easier way. One word of caution with posting your policies online, however: Ensure that links to the policies (and even any links within policies themselves) are kept current. Issues can arise if your organization revamps its website and links to policies become broken. As well as posting policies in PDF or other formats online, a number of organizations are starting to use "microsites" to present the policy in an easier-to-navigate version. Though it requires some financial investment, technology can help ethics and compliance in a variety of ways; it is worth looking into what will be most helpful to your employees, what their preferences are, and what your organization can afford.

2. **App:** Do you recall the Apple advert from 2009 featuring the phrase "there's an app for that"? It felt like nearly every meeting back in the early 2010s inevitably involved someone informing the room that there was an app for absolutely everything. While apps are still very popular at the time of writing (or perhaps they are not, and that is a sign that I am not young and cool anymore), I generally urge caution when I hear organizations wanting to create an app to make their policies and other elements of their ethics and compliance program available to employees. Many codes of conduct are still 50 pages (or longer), and viewing a 50-page document on a phone app is not user friendly in my opinion. Creating and hosting an app can be expensive, and I think an organization would need to have a high degree of certainty that employees would actually download, use, and find the app to be useful before making such a significant investment of money and time. In most instances, I would recommend skipping the app idea and focusing on other ways to make policies accessible to employees.

3. **Intranet or Policy Platform:** Many organizations have internal websites (intranets) that host various materials and other documents

for employees. These intranet sites can be a good place for housing policies, provided they are clearly labeled and stored in a place where employees could logically find them. Another option to consider is a third-party policy platform the organization can purchase or subscribe to. Policy platforms can be useful for employees and also provide actionable, useful data for the ethics and compliance team to understand which policies—and even which sections of policies—are reviewed the most. The downside to storing policies on intranet pages or policy platforms is that employees will need to be logged in to access them; this can add to the amount of time it takes to find a policy, and some employees (particularly if they do not have their own computer issued by the organization) may not regularly log in to these systems. If policies are made available in various locations and formats (e.g., the internet, an intranet page, a policy platform, and in hard copy), it can make for less reliable data on how employees use the policies. Large organizations with employees in multiple countries also need to consider if employees in one country can access the intranet page and whether the policies need to be stored on a local intranet page or somehow otherwise made available to those employees.

4. **To Print or Not to Print?:** As we move to an increasingly digital world focused on sustainability, there will be less need and demand to physically print policies (which is also expensive). I still find that some countries around the world have a strong preference for printed versions of certain policies; those cultural norms should be considered and respected. For the organizations that continue to embrace "hybrid working" and for those employees who do not have a desk or place to store policies (in retail and manufacturing, for example), printed policies may be of limited value. Before printing a new policy, I recommend consulting with the relevant employee base to determine if a printed version would be useful. You might also monitor the

recycling containers on the days following a policy launch to see if those newly printed policies have ended up there.

5. **Making Policies Available in Multiple Locations:** There is some value in making policies available in multiple ways, especially if different employees have different preferences. The key here is managing version control. It is worthwhile to keep a record of where different policies are stored to ensure that dated policies are replaced with newer versions and that multiple versions of a policy are not all available at one location.

Avoid Sunk Cost Bias

Drafting, socializing, and launching policies can take a long time and require a significant amount of work. Even if you follow all the steps in this chapter, there is always a chance that a policy you create may not work as intended or that something may change in the organization, causing the policy to be outdated or less than ideal. You might hear complaints from employees about the policy, particularly if it required transformational rather than incremental change and if there was a lack of effective change management. You might also see other indications that the policy has failed to live up to expectations (for example, online testing indicates employees do not understand the policy, audit findings reveal control or other failures, or helpline or other speak-up data reveals trends that suggest employees are not complying with the policy).

After all the work you have put into creating a policy, the last thing you want is to realize you need to change course and rethink the entire policy. This is indeed frustrating, but we have to remember that policies are only intended as tools to help other people; if the policy is not helping other people do what is expected and/or protecting people from harm by others, then the policy is not worth clinging to. The sunk cost bias can cause us to continue going down a path due solely to the amount of time and effort we've already dedicated to the effort;

however, if a policy is not working, your organization should not be afraid to re-think the policy and start over again. A best-in-class policy (if there is such a thing) is of little value if the written policy and the policy in practice are two very different things.

Is your organization mindful about whether new or updated policies are aiming to drive incremental or transformational change?

I've had several conversations recently about change management, and I enjoyed reading about incremental versus transformational change in Lisa Beth Lentini Walker and Stef Tschida's book, *Raise Your Game, Not Your Voice*.[33] It got me thinking about how new or updated policies can either bring about incremental or transformational change, and why it is so important for ethics and compliance professionals to be aware of the change new or updated policies bring (or hope to bring), and to what degree. Sometimes big, transformational changes are needed, but those can be hard to introduce in a way that will be received well and followed in practice. Policies that introduce incremental change can be easier to roll out and effective in getting people to change their behaviors, but they may not be appropriate if big changes are needed. Neither is necessarily right or wrong, but it is important to understand what change and how much is desired (and likely to be achieved), as well as how to achieve the change in a way that employees won't resent. What may seem like an incremental change to the policy drafter may in fact result in transformational change for employees who need to comply with the policy. Be sure to socialize policies with employees who will be impacted and get their feedback (and, hopefully, their buy-in) to decide whether you should pursue incremental or transformational change with your policies.

---

[33] Lisa Beth Lentini Walker and Stef Tschida, *Raise Your Game, Not Your Voice: How Listening, Communicating, and Storytelling Shape Compliance Program Influence*. Dallas: (CCI Press, 2021).

7 TIPS FOR LAUNCHING NEW ETHICS & COMPLIANCE POLICIES

1 — ASSUME NOT EVERYONE WILL READ THE POLICY

IT DOESN'T MATTER HOW MANY HOURS YOU PUT INTO WRITING THE POLICY, YOU SHOULD ASSUME THAT A GOOD PERCENTAGE OF YOUR EMPLOYEES HAVE LITTLE DESIRE AND INTEREST TO READ A POLICY. SOME PEOPLE MIGHT READ/SKIM THE POLICY, BUT DON'T ASSUME EVERYONE WILL AND YOU NEED TO FIND OTHER WAYS TO CONNECT WITH PEOPLE. SPORTS FANS (AND OFTEN PLAYERS TOO) LEARN THE RULES OF THEIR SPORT NOT FROM RULE BOOKS, BUT FROM PLAYING/EXPERIENCING THE GAME AND TALKING WITH OTHER PEOPLE.

2 — MARKET THE POLICY

TREAT POLICIES LIKE A NEW PRODUCT LAUNCH AND DESIGN A MARKETING CAMPAIGN FOR THE TARGET AUDIENCE(S) IN WAYS THAT ARE RELEVANT AND RESONATE. SIMPLY MAKING PEOPLE AWARE OF YOUR POLICY IS NOT ENOUGH; BRAND RELEVANCE AND RESONANCE ARE WHAT MATTER. THIS CAN INCLUDE SHORT MESSAGES, VIDEO MESSAGES, DIGITAL COMMUNICATIONS, ENDORSEMENTS FROM LEADERS ABOUT THE POLICY IN THEIR MEETINGS – DON'T JUST CREATE NOISE, FIND WAYS TO MARKET THE POLICY EFFECTIVELY AND CONNECT PEOPLE TO THE PRINCIPLES BEHIND IT.

3 — EXPLAIN WHY YOU NEED THE POLICY

THIS SHOULD BE CLEARLY ADDRESSED IN THE POLICY ITSELF (AND, IDEALLY, NOT SIMPLY "WE HAVE THIS POLICY BECAUSE A REGULATOR EXPECTS US TO" – THAT WILL ENGAGE NO ONE AND SAYS YOUR PROGRAM IS ONLY ABOUT AVOIDING LIABILITY FOR THE ORGANIZATION AND NOT ADDING VALUE OR HELPING PEOPLE). IF YOU CAN'T GIVE A REAL REASON WHY YOU HAVE A POLICY AND THE VALUE IT ADDS, YOU ARE GOING TO HAVE A TOUGH TIME GETTING PEOPLE TO ENGAGE AND COMPLY.

4 — USE ACTUAL FAQS

FAQS THAT ARE ACTUAL QUESTIONS FROM EMPLOYEES WHO ARE COVERED BY, OR OTHERWISE IMPACTED BY, THE POLICY CAN HELP HIGHLIGHT THE PRINCIPLES IN REAL HUMAN TERMS AND STORIES (GATHER THESE QUESTIONS WHEN SOCIALIZING THE DRAFT POLICY OR QUESTIONS TO PRIOR VERSIONS OR RELATED POLICIES). FAQS THAT ARE SIMPLY REPEATING THE POLICY ITSELF ARE NOT HELPFUL.

5 — AWKWARD IS MY SPECIALTY

KNOW THE UNCOMFORTABLE SITUATIONS THAT THIS POLICY MIGHT PUT PEOPLE IN. ANTICIPATE THOSE SITUATIONS, OPENLY AND PROACTIVELY ACKNOWLEDGE THEM AND, IF POSSIBLE, DO SOMETHING TO HELP WITH THE AWKWARDNESS. (THE TITLE OF THIS ONE IS TAKEN FROM MY FAVORITE COFFEE MUG)

6 — INTENT VERSUS IMPACT

AFTER LAUNCHING AND MARKETING THE POLICY, SPEAK WITH PEOPLE WHO SHOULD BE KNOWLEDGEABLE ABOUT THE POLICY OR THAT IT SHOULD OTHERWISE IMPACT THEM IN SOME WAY. ARE THE MARKETING AND COMMUNICATION EFFORTS WORKING? IS THE IMPACT OF THE POLICY THE SAME AS THE INTENT? IS THE POLICY IN PRACTICE THE SAME AS THE WRITTEN POLICY?

7 — AVOID SUNK COST BIAS

IF A POLICY IS NOT WORKING, THEN YOU MIGHT NEED TO RE-WRITE OR RE-THINK IT. IT'S MUCH BETTER TO SAY "WE HEARD THE FEEDBACK" RATHER THAN CONTINUING A POLICY THAT IS NOT ADDING VALUE OR HELPING ANYONE. THERE IS NO SUCH THING AS A PERFECT POLICY; INSTEAD, AIM FOR A POLICY THAT SUPPORTS PROGRESS FOR YOUR ETHICS AND COMPLIANCE PROGRAM.

#ETHICSANDCOMPLIANCEFORHUMANS   #SUNDAYMORNINGCOMPLIANCETIP

ADAM BALFOUR

CHAPTER 11

A LETTER TO YOUR ORGANIZATION'S LEADERS, MANAGERS, AND SUPERVISORS

Leaders, managers, and supervisors play a key role in supporting ethics and compliance programs for humans. Use this chapter to learn how to engage the leaders, managers, and supervisors in your organization – or ask them to read it.

Do leaders, managers, and supervisors in your organization say, "Ethics and compliance are important; that's a given," but then move on?

Sales and profits are "a given," and they are continuously discussed, analyzed, measured, and incentivized. Saying the importance of ethics and compliance is "a given" is not enough. Leaders, managers, and supervisors need to be willing, on a regular and ongoing basis, to explain why ethics and compliance matter and what that means in practice for employees. The message doesn't need to be long, profound, or complex—but it must be genuine and sincere. Many things in life are important and should be "a given;" we make them so by talking about them on a regular basis and helping people understand their importance.

The words of leaders matter. Leaders set the tone for the rest of the organization, influencing and (ideally) cascading the expectations and culture of integrity throughout the organization while framing ethics and compliance in relevant terms that will resonate for employees.

But in order for leadership engagement to be effective—and perceived as effective—by the rest of the organization, it must be genuine. Employees can easily see through scripted speeches and tell when leaders' words are inconsistent with their actions and what they allow.

Leadership not only sets the organization's direction and priorities, but also plays a vital role in ensuring objectives are met in accordance with the organization's standards and values.

Achieving results often requires the leader to inspire, guide, and coach. Given that the Center for Creative Leadership has found that 20% of adult learning occurs through coaching, and developmental relationships, this provides an opportunity to drive home the importance of integrity and doing the right thing.[39] Sometimes this will involve providing feedback to employees when they have done the right thing (especially if doing so was difficult); sometimes it will involve having a difficult conversation when someone's behavior falls short of expectations.

This type of coaching and feedback supports organizational values and culture and provides employees with feedback to help them grow and learn. Difficult conversations are never fun, but helping employees learn and grow for the future is part of a leader's job.

Leadership roles are not for everyone; it is both hard at times and probably one of the best professional privileges I have had, because leadership, like ethics and compliance, is an opportunity to help your employees so that your organization can live up to its mission and purpose. And it's bigger than that, as your leadership can help ensure that your communities, near and far, benefit from your collective work and are not harmed by the acts or omissions of people under your responsibility.

Perhaps you bought this book or were asked to read this chapter by a colleague who works in ethics and compliance. Whatever the reason, I hope you know that you have an opportunity to use your position, voice, and influence to have a lasting impact. You have a key role in ensuring your organization has an effective culture of integrity.

> **"** *Employees can easily see through scripted speeches and tell when leaders' words are inconsistent with their actions and what they allow.* **"**

Ethics and compliance can seem like an abstract concept. This chapter might not provide all the answers to your questions, but I hope it will give you some ideas as to how to help your fellow employees and help ensure your organization lives up to its purpose and acts with integrity.

Do Leaders, Managers, and Supervisors Actually Know What's Expected of Them?

Tone at the top (which certainly has to be more than empty words or "CEO letters" that everyone knows were never written by the CEO) is a key expectation of regulators and has been described by Deloitte as "first ingredient in building a world-class ethics and compliance program." [34]

Many organizations recognize this, and with good intentions they set expectations for leaders, managers, and supervisors by describing them as a reporting channel—often employees' preferred reporting channel—and also by saying things in the code of conduct such as:

> **"As a leader, you have a special responsibility for setting the culture and the work environment on your team."**

> **"While all employees must always act with integrity, each manager and leader has the increased responsibility to lead by example and empower others to deliver by reinforcing the principles of our code throughout all levels of our workforce."**

These are all good statements, and one would hope they are reflective of reality, but do most leaders really know what they need to do to live up to their "special responsibility" and "increased responsibility?" These fairly unclear responsibilities will create expectations in the minds of most employees about the knowledge and resourcefulness of their leader, manager, or supervisor, but without actually helping leaders know what is expected of them, we are letting everyone involved down.

---

[34] "Tone at the top: The first ingredient in a world-class ethics and compliance program," Deloitte, September 2014, https://www2.deloitte.com/content/dam/Deloitte/us/Documents/risk/us-aers-tone-at-the-top-sept-2014.pdf.

If your organization creates an expectation for employees that leaders, managers, and supervisors are their primary source of guidance on ethics and compliance issues, then making the responsibilities clear and easy to understand will not only directly support the leaders, managers, and supervisors, it will also support the rest of the organization. At the very least, leaders need to learn what type of ethics and compliance situations they are likely to face and how to handle them. Here are some time-tested, practical ways we can make their role and responsibilities less scary and abstract:

Meeting With Leaders: A one-on-one meeting between a people manager and someone from the ethics and compliance team is an excellent use of time to explain the program and the leader's role in it while getting their feedback on what is and isn't working with the program. While leaders and managers often have little time (and many competing demands for that time), this type of meeting can be an hour-long private conversation in which the leader or manager can ask any questions that they might not otherwise be comfortable asking. This can include discussion around what a specific manager or leader should be doing and how they can support ethics and compliance. These conversations can help build trust and communication so that the leader or manager feels the ethics and compliance team is there to help.

Compliance Manager Tool Kits: With tight schedules in mind, I have found it's useful to periodically create and roll out "compliance manager tool kits" that address specific situations or behaviors and provide practical guidance. I attach a title to these tool kits that clearly captures the topic in ten words or so. For instance,

- *"How to Talk About Ethics and Compliance With Your Team,"*

- *"What to Do if Someone Raises a Compliance Concern to You,"*

- *"How to Help Your New Hire Understand the Ethics and Compliance Program,"*

- *"Four Things Leaders and Managers Can Do to Drive a Culture of Integrity,"* or

- *"How to Help Employees Navigate the Policy on Gifts, Meals, Entertainment, and Travel to and From Third Parties."*

The tool kits are designed to be visually appealing, ideally consistent with other organizational branding materials, and quick and easy reads. They explain in five or so points what specific things a leader, manager, or supervisor should do or not do in a particular situation. While many of the tool kits are likely common sense to most ethics and compliance professionals, we should not take for granted that all leaders, managers, or supervisors will necessarily know what they should do or how they can help their teams. An example of a tool kit is the "Ethical Leadership to Do List" included at the end of this chapter.

The Problem with Pressure

It's clear that you have a responsibility to set the ethical tone at your organization, but you also have a responsibility to achieve bottom-line results. And as we know, achieving results can often involve people working under pressure. Pressure is not inherently bad; the right type and amount of pressure can help us, both individually and collectively, to achieve more than we otherwise would. Pressure can motivate and benefit those under pressure, as well as leading to good outcomes, but unchecked pressure or pressure to achieve results at the expense of ethics and the law can wreak havoc.

A 2020 Global Business Ethics Survey found that "globally, more than 1 in every 5 employees feel pressure to compromise their organization's ethics standards, policies, or the law," and that pressure was felt by an even higher percentage of people in North America (31%) and South America (37%).

> **“** *If your organization creates an expectation for employees that leaders, managers, and supervisors are their primary source of guidance on ethics and compliance issues, then making the responsibilities clear and easy to understand will not only directly support the leaders, managers, and supervisors, it will also support the rest of the organization.* **”**

As a leader, you play a critical role in ensuring that the level of pressure does not become too much and that the pressure to achieve organizational goals does not come at the expense of ethical standards or policies or lead to anyone violating the law. This is not a theoretical point. In February 2020, Wells Fargo "agreed to pay $3 billion to resolve their potential criminal and civil liability stemming from a practice between 2002 and 2016 of pressuring employees to meet unrealistic sales goals that led thousands of employees to provide millions of accounts or products to customers under false pretenses or without consent." As then-current U.S. Attorney Nick Hanna for the Central District of California said, "[t]his case illustrates a complete failure of leadership at multiple levels within the Bank."

This matter is a reminder for us all that leaders, managers, and supervisors at all levels must be engaged in ensuring a culture of ethics and integrity in everything your employees and organization do.

Does an Effective Ethics and Compliance Program Really Increase Revenue or Otherwise Financially Support the Organization?

It is not uncommon now to see penalties and fines for ethics and compliance violations into the billions of U.S. dollars. Ethics and compliance violations can also result in significant legal and other costs (in 2019, Walmart was fined $282 million for bribery and paid approximately $1 billion in legal fees and other costs), and other organizations have also seen their share price drop significantly due to compliance issues (Luckin Coffee's share price dropped from $50 a share to $1.39 a share in a very short period of time in 2019 following an accounting and sales fraud scandal that also resulted in their CEO and COO being fired).

While an effective ethics and compliance program can help avoid fines, penalties, and other negative financial and reputational impacts, these programs can also add significant value to the organization by way of fewer lawsuits, smaller settlements, and even higher profits.

"I Don't Feel Comfortable Talking About Ethics and Compliance. What If I Don't Say Whatever I Need to Say in a Perfect Way?"

Effective communication is not only based on what is communicated, but also who is communicating the message and to whom the message is communicated. Think about when Jerry Seinfeld tells a joke and how that compares with you or I trying to retell the same joke. The same words land completely differently because of who is sending the message and how they communicate it.

Of course, you should regularly reach out and rely on your ethics and compliance team for support (if they are not already doing so, they will soon be providing you and other leaders a Compliance Tip of the Month that you can easily talk about with your team in just a few minutes). But your employees will also benefit by hearing you regularly talk about the importance of ethics and compliance and framing the message in a way that is relevant to and resonates with your team. To have an impact on employees, your message doesn't have to be "perfect," it just needs to be sincere.

You have influence, and your voice is heard differently when compared with others in the organization, including the ethics and compliance team. You can make a real difference in how employees see you as a leader and how they believe in the organization when you regularly talk about ethics and compliance with them.

You can talk about ethics and compliance in a variety of ways, including through more formal communication at least once a month in team meetings and by informally working ethics and compliance into one-on-one and daily conversations. You can also talk to new hires about what ethics and compliance means at your organization and in your team, as well as the different resources available to them. Other topics you can cover include relevant news headlines (especially those relating to your industry or customers), real-world examples, and lessons from within the organization or your own career; these examples and stories can help bring ethics and compliance to life for your team.

"We Have an Ethics Hotline. Can't I Just Encourage People to Use it Rather than Raising Matters to Me?"

Speaking up might be the right thing to do in many occasions, but it isn't always easy and can be very comfortable for a lot of people. It might be difficult for someone to talk about ill treatment, whether their own or someone else's. They could be worried about whether they will be believed or if anything will be done. They could be worried that they are mistaken or that they are going to get someone else into trouble. They could be worried that you will think differently about them or view them as not being "a team player" by speaking up. There are so many reasons someone might find it difficult to speak up, but you can help them.

Employees should have a variety of ways to raise concerns, ask questions, or report suspected and actual wrongdoing, and they should use the speak-up channel they feel most comfortable with.

An Anonymous Ethics Helpline Should Not Be The Only Way Employees Can Raise Concerns Or Seek Help.

While a leader may have good intentions by always directing employees to report through a helpline and by reminding people that doing so can be done anonymously, if that's the only speak-up messaging an employee hears, you may inadvertently be communicating (a) we rely on a third-party hotline provider because it's not safe or effective to speak up directly in the organization, and (b) if you're going to speak up, don't be an idiot and tell us who you are.

In some instances, reporting anonymously through the ethics helpline might be an individual's preferred approach, and we should leave the decision on how to raise a concern to the individual employee. But the hotline cannot be employees' only option. Make sure your regularly remind employees that speaking up is encouraged and that they have multiple ways to seek help.

If An Employee Comes To You For Help, It Is A Sign They Trust You.

Telling the person to "go call the hotline" can have a negative impact on employees and make them question whether you're really supportive of them. If someone raises a concern to you, take the time to listen, show empathy, and take their concerns seriously. As you gather information, you'll develop a sense of whether they are holding back any additional information due to fear of retaliation, worries about incriminating others, or concerns about how you will perceive them. As you listen closely to the person's story (which might include their perceptions, judgments, and emotions), you will be helping your organization and your employee.

Once someone has raised a matter to you, they do not need to then report it again through the ethics helpline. At that point, it's on you, as the leader, manager, or supervisor, to engage the right department or function (Internal Audit, Compliance, Human Resources, Legal, etc.) to determine next steps.

You must thank the person who spoke up and reinforce that you value them for doing so. Although you might not be able to share with them any details of a subsequent investigation, you can still "close the loop" with the employee by expressing gratitude for their courage and by making sure the person felt heard.

It's worth remembering that something might appear small from the organization's perspective, but the matter may be of great significance to the individual. Treating both employees and the information they're sharing as meaningful makes a real difference in this process. If an important customer was having issues or concerns about your organization's offerings or services, you would hope to hear about it (and have the chance to address their concerns) before they tell you that they are going to another provider or filing a lawsuit. The same is true with your employees; if they are facing issues or have concerns, it is better for everyone that they tell you early on so you have the chance to address their concerns, rather than your becoming aware of the issue only when they leave for another job or file a lawsuit. Remember too: Speaking up is a sign of a healthy organizational culture, and your reactions play a critical role in creating and supporting that culture. How you handle the situation can either reinforce and strengthen that trust, or it can irrevocably damage it.

"I'm Already Working 60+ Hours, So Your Suggestions Cannot Take a Lot of My Time."

This doesn't have to be a time-consuming effort. These are the most important things you can do:

- **Use your voice** by regularly talking about the importance and relevance of ethics and integrity with your team and any new hires.

- **Provide feedback** both when employees exceed and when they fall below expectations when it comes to integrity.

- **Promote the resources available** to support employees (and where to find them), including the code of conduct and the various speak-up channels.

- **Be an example** by following organizational standards and living the organizational values (including speaking up), as well as promptly completing requirements such as online training or certifications.

- **Proactively build trust** with your team by sharing stories of the ethical dilemmas you have faced in your career and regularly asking them if they have any concerns or matters they would like to discuss or need guidance on.

- **Be genuine and confident** in knowing which matters you can handle and which you need to engage other people to help with.

None of these items, individually or collectively, will require a significant amount of your time. Of course, your colleague(s) in ethics and compliance are here to help you, as well.

The next page captures these action items in a simple "Ethical Leadership to Do List." To excel as a leader, consult it regularly as a way to maintain trust with your team and ensure you are helping your colleagues act with integrity.

You are no doubt already doing many of these things. To those of you who lead with integrity, thank you. What you do matters.

Ethical Leadership
TO DO LIST

- [ ] TALK ABOUT ETHICS AND COMPLIANCE WITH MY TEAM AT LEAST ONCE A MONTH.

- [ ] TALK TO NEW HIRES TO MAKE SURE THEY KNOW HOW TO SPEAK UP, WHERE TO FIND THE CODE OF CONDUCT AND WHY INTEGRITY MATTERS.

- [ ] MAKE SURE MY TEAM AND I COMPLETE ANY REQUIRED ACTIONS (ONLINE COURSES, LIVE TRAININGS OR DISCLOSURE CERTIFICATIONS) IN A TIMELY MANNER.

- [ ] REGULARLY AND PROACTIVELY ASK MY TEAM DURING 1-1'S IF THEY HAVE CONCERNS OR KNOW OF ANY ETHICAL MATTERS THAT WE SHOULD DISCUSS (DON'T WAIT FOR PEOPLE TO SPEAK UP - START THE CONVERSATION).

- [ ] THANK SOMEONE WHEN THEY SPEAK UP, SHOW CARE AND MAKE SURE MATTER IS LOOKED INTO AND CLOSURE PROVIDED TO PERSON WHO SPOKE UP.

- [ ] GET COMFORTABLE WITH KNOWING I WON'T HAVE ALL THE ANSWERS AND REACH OUT TO OTHERS IN THE ORGANIZATION FOR HELP AND GUIDANCE AS NEEDED.

- [ ] LEAD BY EXAMPLE, INCLUDING SPEAKING UP AND DEMONSTRATING INTEGRITY EVEN IF DOING SO IS HARD.

ADAM BALFOUR

CONCLUSION:
TOWARD A CHIEF PURPOSE OFFICER

From Public Statements to Living Your Organizational Purpose

Many organizations have a stated purpose that directly ties in with and impacts the organization's brand. Often that purpose is to help humanity and the world. Take for instance:

JETBLUE: "To inspire humanity—both in the air and on the ground."

ASANA: "To help humanity thrive by enabling all teams to work together effortlessly."

PATAGONIA: "Build the best product, cause no unnecessary harm, use business to inspire, and implement solutions to the environmental crisis."

SEVENTH GENERATION: "To provid[e] effective, safe, bio-based products that are good for the planet and for your family. ... to create a more healthy, sustainable and equitable world for the generations to come."

THE RED CROSS: "To protect life and health and to ensure respect for the human being."

TOMS: "To use business to improve lives."

ALLBIRDS: "To prove that comfort, good design, and sustainability don't have to be mutually exclusive."

VIRGIN: "To change business for good."

When purpose-driven organizations genuinely commit to their purpose, it helps align employees' behavior and the organization's priorities, and it provides a moral and ethical measuring stick and compass to guide strategy and decisions.

In recent years, Patagonia has been held as the model example of an organization that intentionally and obsessively pursues its purpose. Among various other acts consistent with its purpose and values (including the 2011 marketing campaign that placed an advert in The New York Times during Black Friday with a picture of a Patagonia jacket that said "DON'T BUY THIS JACKET"), in 2022, Yvon Chouinard announced that he was transferring 100% of the company's voting stock to the Patagonia Purpose Trust "to protect the company's values," as well as 100% of the non-voting stock to Holdfast Collective, signaling that "Earth is now our only shareholder." [35] These acts very much reflect Patagonia's stated values to "build the best product," to "seek not only to do less harm, but more good," and to "not [be] bound by convention." [36]

At the same time, there are many examples of companies that have made public statements that were very much at odds with their actual practices. The story of Enron's collapse is one that remains relevant more than two decades later.

Enron had an ethics and compliance program. It had a code of conduct that ran over 60 pages in length, covered topics such as human rights and business ethics, and described elements of Enron's antitrust and anticorruption programs. The Code included a letter from then-Chairman and CEO, Kenneth Lay, encouraging "all officers and employees of Enron Corp., its subsidiaries, and its affiliated companies" to conduct "the business affairs of the companies in accordance with all applicable laws and in a moral and honest manner." The company's core values of respect, integrity, communication, and excellence were even carved in marble in the lobby of its headquarters. Enron had a stated vision of becoming "the world's leading energy company—creating innovative and efficient energy solutions for growing economies and a better environment worldwide." As we now know, Enron filed for bankruptcy after it was revealed

---

[35] Yvon Chouinard, "Earth is now our only shareholder," Patagonia, https://www.patagonia.com/ownership/.

[36] "Our Core Values," Patagonia, https://www.patagonia.com/core-values/.

that fraudulent and irregular accounting practices were rampant and even involved the now-defunct auditing firm of Arthur Andersen.

Clearly, stating a commitment to "Integrity"—and even carving it in stone— is very different from acting with integrity and living those values and organizational purpose.

On the Topic of Trust

While the magnitude of the Enron scandal means that it is still relevant and discussed more than twenty years later, there have since been countless other examples in which stated integrity has not been reflected in an organization's actions and practices, nor in the behavior of its employees. The result? Trust issues.

Each year, Edelman, a global public relations consultancy firm, issues their Trust Barometer Report, which includes data and public perceptions about the state of trust around the world. Edelman describes trust as "the ultimate currency in the relationship that all institutions—business, governments, NGOs, and media— build with their stakeholders." [43]

I find this report to be very relevant to ethics and compliance professionals, since trust can be a driving force in helping people act in ethical and compliant ways. Trust is fundamental in encouraging people who have been harmed or who are aware of wrongdoing to speak up, and it is also important in terms of how customers, consumers, employees, shareholders, and others view the organization, its products and services, and its brand.

The Edelman report has also shown that social pressures on and expectations of organizations are increasing, and they're likely to continue increasing. Yet we live in an era of relatively low trust. One of the headlines from the 2022 report reads, "FAILURE OF LEADERSHIP MAKES DISTRUST THE DEFAULT."

---

[43] "2022 Edelman Trust Barometer: The Cycle of Distrust," Edelman.com, 2022, https://www.edelman. com/trust/2022-trust-barometer.

Distrust in each other and in institutions such as businesses, governments, and the media is worrying, though it provides an opportunity for those organizations that seek to genuinely act in a trustworthy way with their employees, their customers, other business partners, and the world at large—but this will require strong, purpose-driven leadership.

While we are certainly facing challenging times, there are opportunities for organizations—particularly businesses—to renew trust and help society. The Edelman Trust Barometer Report has shown that increasing numbers of people "want more, not less, business engagement on societal issues," that businesses are seen as both more competent and ethical than governments and the media, that 58% of people "buy or advocate for brands based on their beliefs and values," that 60% of people "choose a place to work based on their beliefs and values," and that 64% of people "invest based on their beliefs and values."

As we discussed in the previous chapter, ethical leadership requires intentional effort, but leaders, managers, and supervisors have the power and influence to build and sustain trust and integrity within organizations. Trust, integrity, and purpose-driven leadership can come together to make for more engaging, psychologically safer, and more inclusive places of work; to earn and maintain the trust of customers and consumers; and to be a force for societal good while also delivering strong financial results for organizations and stakeholders.

But in order for this to happen, we have to be intentional about how our organizations demonstrate a commitment to trust, integrity, and purpose-driven leadership. For further reading on this point, I highly recommend the book Intentional Integrity: How Smart Companies Can Lead An Ethical Revolution, by Rob Chesnut, former General Counsel and Chief Ethics Officer at Airbnb, as he details why and how organizations can successfully be intentional in these areas.

Aligning the Purpose-Driving Functions: Toward the Chief Purpose Officer

Although ESG (environmental, social, and governance) is not a new concept, it is being looked at in new ways, and it has become a hot topic in recent years. Based on Google Trends data from the period of January 1, 2004 to December 2022, the term "ESG" began a significant upward trend starting in 2019 and has remained high ever since. Concerns about the environment, social pressures, governance, sustainability, diversity, privacy, volatility in the world, and integrity have led organizations to consider the ways they operate and evaluate whether and how to change to meet present and future social expectations. Stakeholders, including regulators, employees, consumers, investors, and others, are carefully watching and scrutinizing to see if an organization's words match its actions. This quickly separates organizations that are greenwashing and making empty statements from those that are seeking to build trust, act with integrity, and demonstrate purpose-driven leadership.

As organizations continue to evaluate their purpose, and as social pressures and investors continue to closely monitor an organization's commitment to that purpose, I believe there will be an ever-increasing need for alignment among those functions in order to manage trust with stakeholders (including ethics and compliance) and guide the organization's priorities and its employees' behaviors. These different internal functions can add even more value if they are united in helping people pursue the organizational purpose.

My hope for the near future is that we will see the rise and emergence of the Chief Purpose Officer among the top ranks of the C-Suite. Although there are a small number of organizations with a Chief Purpose Officer today, I am not aware of any large organization in which this is one of the main C-Suite roles and where this leader has significant influence in the organization's strategic decision-making and priorities. Ideally, the Chief Purpose Officer would be charged with ensuring that the organization, its employees, and their individual and collective acts both align with and advance the organization's purpose, as well as seeking to build trust within and outside the organization and acting with integrity in everything they do. There is a lot of pressure on organizations to take stances on various social issues and a smart, experienced and informed Chief Purpose Officer could help guide an organization to take an affirmative stance on these issues that are core and relevant to an organization's purpose and not try to appease on other social issues. All the internal functions that help to manage trust with internal and external stakeholders (including ethics and compliance, human-focused HR departments, and other similar groups such as DEI, sustainability, and ESG for some organizations) should report into the Chief Purpose Officer to drive the organization ever closer toward its purpose and to adapt as societal and market expectations evolve. Other C-Suite members, who also play an important role in supporting the organizational purpose, would likewise ensure the organization's unwavering commitment to purpose; add short- and long-term financial, brand, and reputational value; and ensure the organization's focus on its positive impact. While many CEOs and other C-Suite leaders are purpose-driven, a Chief Purpose Officer can operate as the internal Supreme Court, interpreting and protecting the organization's constitutional purpose. Pressure will—and to some extent should—always exist in organizations, and having the C-Suite obsess about purpose and integrity will help ensure that the pressure to achieve financial results does not come at the expense of trust, integrity, people, or the planet. As we have discussed in earlier chapters, a strong and genuine commitment to and investment in ethics and compliance supports an organization's short- and long-term financial success. We need trust, integrity, and purpose-driven leadership to become the default, and we can start by building ethics and compliance programs for humans.

The moments that go into the history books often involve the worst or the best of human behavior. Whether we are warring and killing each other, creating medicines that save or enhance the quality and longevity of human lives, turning a blind eye to abuse of others, coming together through sports to test and push our human limits, allowing bribery and corruption to run rampant, or creating technologies and innovations that change the world and human experience (for better or for worse), our biggest impacts on the world and history swing between the extremes of the darkest and brightest aspects of humanity and human nature.

My hope is that building effective ethics and compliance programs for humans can give the upper hand, with future history books showcasing more stories of human behavior at its finest rather than at its worst. Creating ethics and compliance programs for humans means not only making these programs better suited for humans in terms of how we see and interact with our organizational ethics and compliance programs, but also making the outcomes more effective and more human.

Finally, I would be doing a disservice to my many colleagues, friends, and mentors in the ethics and compliance community if I did not close with a note about them and what they do. In an address at Compliance Week 2022, then-Assistant Attorney General Kenneth A. Polite concluded his remarks to an audience of ethics and compliance professionals by describing "how powerful a role you have in improving our corporate culture and improving our world."[37] He described this work as a "calling," which, in my opinion, perfectly describes what drives the ethics and compliance professionals who strive, struggle, persist, care deeply about people and purpose, and continue to make their organizations and the world a little bit better one day at a time.

When you bring together a group of people who share the same "calling," you realize the power of community and how it installs the renewed belief that we can and must encourage the human race to live up to our potential of goodness for ourselves, our planet, and humanity itself (at least it does for me). As I hope this book has shown, our efforts and calling to build and ever improve ethics and compliance programs for humans are aimed at much more than simply avoiding fines and penalties, but instead adding value to the human experience.

---

[37] "Transcript: Kenneth Polite Jr. keynote address at Compliance Week 2022," Compliance Week, 2022, https://www.complianceweek.com/regulatory-enforcement/transcript-kenneth-polite-jr-keynote-address-at-compliance-week-2022/31698.article.

Organizations need to have people working in ethics and compliance who have relevant knowledge and experience, there must be sufficient numbers of people with adequate resources to run and manage these programs, and they must be enabled to influence and be among the organization's highest levels of leaders and decision-makers. The ethics and compliance department should be home to some of the most diverse skill sets of any department in the organization; they need the skills to interpret laws and regulations, design programs, write comprehensible policies and procedures, understand organizational cultures, conduct data analytics, assess risks, help people learn, create engaging content, conduct investigations, and ensure all of this is done in human-centric way.

The role of today's ethics and compliance professionals is a demanding one; they need to have the tools, resources, time, data, people, and technology to support them in their endeavors. While we have repeatedly and regularly heard from regulators on these points, I hope readers will see that making the necessary investments in ethics and compliance programs not only meets regulator expectations and minimizes risk for the organization, but also enables the organization to deliver on its purpose, be financially successful, and guide and protect its people.

ADAM BALFOUR

ADDITIONAL RESOURCES

RESOURCE #1

How to Tell Stories Within Your Organization and Learn From Past Lessons

Surrounded by the Eurasian, North American, Pacific, and Philippine tectonic plates, Japan is often impacted by earthquakes and tsunamis. Although many of these earthquakes are fairly minor, several devastating earthquakes and tsunamis have hit Japan throughout history, including the March 11, 2011 earthquake and tsunami that resulted in a nuclear meltdown in three reactors at the Fukushima Daiichi nuclear facility. The Nuclear Accident Independent Investigation Commission wrote "although triggered by these cataclysmic events, the subsequent accident at the Fukushima Daiichi Nuclear Power Plant cannot be regarded as a natural disaster. It was a profoundly manmade disaster—that could and should have been foreseen and prevented."

Japan's coastline is dotted with century-old "tsunami stones" that are intended to serve as a reminder to future generations about tragedies caused by past earthquakes and tsunamis and the need to learn from past mistakes. One such tsunami stone reads: "High dwellings are the peace and harmony of our descendants. Remember the calamity of the great tsunamis. Do not build any homes below this point." Lessons from the past can be forgotten by losing institutional knowledge and diminished by recency bias. Past issues and failures are learning opportunities, but actual learning has to take place, and lessons must be taught to future generations if they are to avoid the same mistakes.

Every organization has likely faced various issues of wrongdoing at some point. Some such events might result in massive fines and penalties and significant media coverage; others may have had impacts that were less publicized. Telling stories from within your organization cannot change the past, but it can help to shape the future; by ensuring that lessons are learned, employees understand what is expected of them, that the organization acts when wrongdoing occurs, and that people are listened to when they speak up.

The following worksheet is intended to help your organization identify what human stories and lessons can be taken from past issues to positively shape its future.

Ethical Lessons From Your Organization's Past

QUESTION 1: What was the event or wrongdoing that happened, and when did it occur?

_____

_____

_____

_____

_____

_____

QUESTION 2: What was the impact of the event or wrongdoing?

_____

_____

_____

_____

_____

_____

QUESTION 3: What were the root causes or contributing factors that lead to the event or wrongdoing? Was it a unique, one-time event, or could something similar occur again?

_____

_____

_____
_____
_____
_____

QUESTION 4: What improvements or measures were put in place to help prevent or detect similar events or wrongdoing in the future?

_____
_____
_____
_____
_____
_____

QUESTION 5: What learning opportunities does this event or wrongdoing provide?

_____
_____
_____
_____
_____
_____

QUESTION 6: How can those learning opportunities be turned into actual learning? Who needs to learn from this?

_____
_____
_____
_____
_____
_____

QUESTION 7: How will this learning be maintained over time? Will it be covered in training, new hire messages, or otherwise?

_____

_____

_____

_____

_____

_____

QUESTION 8: How will the organization know if it is backsliding on the learning? What can be done to ensure that does not happen?

_____

_____

_____

_____

_____

_____

QUESTION 9: What human stories can be told about this event? Whose stories are they, and to whom should they be communicated?

_____

_____

_____

_____

_____

_____

RESOURCE #2

Further Discussion Questions Inspired by the Star Wars Franchise:

- Did the Jedi leaders talk enough about the importance of integrity? Did they provide Anakin with timely, actionable feedback? Could Anakin have benefitted from a "performance improvement plan?"

- Are Jedi mind tricks ethical? The famous line in Episode IV, "These aren't the Droids you're looking for," was a lie—they absolutely were the Droids the Stormtroopers were looking for. Even if the lie proved beneficial, what example does that set for lying in other situations?

- The different leadership styles in the movies, especially comparing General Leia Organa's style to Darth Vader's style of not questioning leadership ("I find your lack of faith disturbing"), ruling through fear, failing to learn from mistakes (the Death Star failures—where was Internal Audit? There seems to be a complete lack of the three lines of defense in the movies) and zero tolerance for mistakes ("Apology accepted, Captain Needa").

- Undisclosed or improperly managed conflicts of interest, including Anakin turning to the Dark Side, thinking it would save Padme, or Darth Vader not disclosing that Luke was his son. How would things have been different if (a) Anakin talked about his conflicts with someone else and (b) if the Jedi leadership proactively and regularly asked Anakin if they had any concerns or felt pressured?

- Obi-Wan's comment to Anakin, "Be mindful of your thoughts, Anakin. They will betray you," seems like a good warning on the risks of isolated decision-making.

- Master Yoda's warning, "Once you start down the dark path, forever will it dominate your destiny," seems to be a message on the risks of ethical fading. Ethical fading is where standards are continuously pushed and eroded until the standard either no longer exists or changes altogether.

- The Jedi Scrolls (or Sacred Jedi texts) contained a set of teachings and rules intended to guide the Jedi, but they were not readily accessible, as Luke Skywalker had hid them in a uneti tree on the planet of Ahch-To. We saw that Rey used the texts to guide her in the later movies, but there was not a lot of discussion in the earlier movies about the standards. This is a good reminder that it is not enough to have written standards (such as a code of conduct); you need to ensure the written standards and the standards in practice are one and the same. By regularly talking about the expected standards, we can help people learn, understand where compliance with standards could be challenging, and help ensure that the group has an aligned and accurate understanding of the expected behaviors. We also do not know if the Jedi scrolls were written by one or more Jedi lawyers to distance any Jedi who committed wrongdoing or designed to help the Jedi (did they have an ethics and compliance program for Jedi?), nor do we know if any of the Jedi actually and regularly read the scrolls.

RESOURCE #3

Three Made-Up Rappers and the Basics of Antitrust Laws

The following is a piece I created as a way to explain the basics of antitrust laws to non-lawyers. Many will find this an odd piece (because it is), but if it helps, then it works. Even if it inspires other creative explanations of complex topics, I will also count that as working.

Let's pretend there are three made-up rappers who compete against each other to be top of the charts. "Denimem," who wears denim cutoffs a la Dr. Tobias Funke from Arrested Development (which is worth watching, rewatching, and obsessively rewatching), "Jay-Zed," (a British knock-off of Jay-Z, and "Dad-Bod," who acts like he has an eight-pack, but at best has a two-pack ("Tupac")—Dad-bod and a dad joke in one: Nailed it!

At first, competition between the three rappers was intense. Each was producing hit after hit, and radio stations and online streaming platforms played their music nonstop, to the delight of rap fans everywhere.

Tired of the competition, Denimem released a new album called Monopoly, which was guaranteed to be a hit and bring in millions, but he told the radio stations and streaming services they could only play his album if they didn't play any songs of Jay-Zed and Dad-Bod for six months. The radio stations and streaming services agreed, and although listeners were initially excited about Monopoly, they were ultimately disappointed since they could only hear Denimem music, but not music from the other rappers. After Monopoly dropped, Denimem no longer felt the need to release good music; he started releasing songs that no one really liked but continued to listen to since they wanted to hear new rap songs but had no alternatives. Even if Denimem continued to make great songs, rap fans would still be harmed, since they wouldn't have the choice to hear new music by other artists.

Denimem decides to take a six-month break from music after the success of Monopoly. Seeing an opportunity to take advantage of one less rapper in the market, Jay-Zed and Dad-Bod agree that they will set and control the prices of their next albums so as not to compete against each other. Jay-Zed says she will sell her next album, Cartel, for $15.99 (almost double the price of her last album), and Dad-Bod agrees to sell his next album, Price Fixing, for the same price. Rather than letting the market set the price of their albums, Jay-Zed and Dad-Bod colluded on the price at which they would sell their music to the market. Rap fans could have benefited from lower-priced albums if the rappers were competing against each other fairly on price or if there were other reasons the album prices increased, but fans now need to spend more money for overpriced albums. Fans were outraged about this agreement to fix prices; it was just wrong. Although there seems to be an express agreement between the two rappers, there could also be an implied agreement based on their actions.

Dad-Bod's next album is the biggest of his career, coming at career low points for Denimem and Jay-Zed, who just could not produce songs that were popular with rap fans. Dad-Bod's album, All My Money Goes to College Funds, made up 75% of all album sales during a three-month period. Although rap fans wished that Jay-Zed and Denimem could shake off their slumps, they also felt that Dad-Bod was doing nothing wrong and were happy that at least one of the rap stars was producing and releasing awesome music.

Jay-Zed is jealous of Dad-Bod's recent success. She knows she cannot go into Dad-Bod's recording studio to hear what he is writing, so she pays an intern at his recording studio to sneak information to her about Dad-Bod's upcoming album. Word gets out about this scheme, and rap fans are furious with Jay-Zed. She protests and tries to blame the intern, but fans are disappointed that she used a third party to get this information. Jay-Zed admits her mistake and realizes that obtaining competitively sensitive information is wrong, regardless of how you get it.

In a bid to restore peace between the warring rap stars, Denimem, Jay-Zed, and Dad-Bod agree they should divide up the rap fans and target their allotted market share with music for that particular group (Denimem targets Prius- and Leaf-driving rap fans with songs such as "Too Poor to Own a Tesla" and "Going Nowhere Fast or Far." Jay-Zed targets rap fans who are afraid of dogs with songs called "Small Dogs, Big Fears" and "Death Lab." Dad-Bod targets vegan and vegetarian rap fans with songs such as "Lie About How Good You Feel" and "Protein Deficient." (Full disclosure, I currently own a Prius, used to own a Leaf, have a somewhat residual fear of dogs, and was vegetarian and then vegan for a number of years). Each rapper respects the fans allocated to the other rappers and won't produce music or appeal to the two other fan groups. Although the fans have some rap music, they miss the good old days, when multiple rappers playing on different radio stations were competing for their attention.

Denimem, Jay-Zed, and Dad-Bod plan to each release new albums next year, and all want to be number one in the charts. In a bid to be number one at different times, they agree that they will release their albums at different times to try rig the charts. While they all land number 1 chart positions, their bid rigging undermines the competition between them and ultimately hurts rap fans. Not only did they rig the charts, but they also limited their output, purposefully not releasing new songs when one of the other rappers was going for the number 1 spot on the charts.

Competition between the three rappers starts to heat up again, and they start including some vague references to each other in their songs. Dad-Bod ups the ante by saying his next album will be $7.99, but will cost $19.99 plus shipping and a delivery fee for anyone who has bought any albums or songs from Denimem or Jay-Zed. Rap fans are disappointed they are being charged differently for the exact same product and do not like the price discrimination for the same commodity. The other rappers follow suit, and rap fans are left short-changed buying differently priced albums.

After a chance encounter at Whole Foods, Denimem, Jay-Zed, and Dad-Bod decide to collaborate on a song called "Sherman," which becomes a huge hit. Fans cannot get enough of it, and the song racks up sales of 1,890 copies the first day. They later collaborate on another song called "Clayton 1914," which is later remixed by DJ Robinson-Patman. This collaboration was great for rap fans and rap music, and there was hope of additional collaborations going forward. Denimem and Dad-Bod thought about joining forces long term to team up against Jay-Zed and limit her ability to compete against them, but they realized that would ultimately harm rap music and fans by having fewer rap stars competing, so they decided against it.

Before their collaboration on "Sherman," Denimem, Jay-Zed, and Dad-Bod were constantly poaching each other's sound engineers; they would google the names of sound engineers on their Apple computers to get intel on who was good and who they should try to poach. (There was a significant antitrust matter involving Google, Apple, Intel and Adobe many years ago, but I couldn't figure out a good way to naturally mention Adobe). The rappers decide to come to an agreement that they won't hire each other's sound engineers anymore. The sound engineers still have jobs, but they aren't able to get the pay raises they used to from hopping from one rapper to another and now feel trapped in their jobs. The sound engineers feel hurt by the rappers they have supported for so long and are stuck using free versions of Adobe (got it) because they do not have enough money to buy the fancier versions of Adobe. (Twice! I'm so good at this.)

Denimem, Jay-Zed, and Dad-Bod, together with some other cool rappers that I couldn't be bothered to invent fake names for, form a rap music association and hold regular meetings. They are well aware of the optics of having competing rap stars meet behind closed doors and want to reassure rap fans and the music industry that these discussions are for pro-competitive purposes. They agree that every meeting will have a written agenda of legitimate topics they can discuss, they will remind themselves (or see if they can get a really cool lawyer who can rap an antitrust admonishment) of the obvious (they won't talk about inappropriate topics or have express or implied agreements not to compete), and they will stick to the agenda and take minutes to reflect what was discussed or rapped. They know they need to be careful with what they say and that words and phrases might have a legitimate intent but can have different meanings or be interpreted differently with hindsight or if someone is missing context (just like the lyrics in their songs). They agree the rap music association can discuss topics such as the lobbying of the music industry for fair pay and treatment for artists, technology for use in rap music, health and safety standards for concerts, the impact of curse words on young children, reducing references to guns and violence, and how to make the rap industry more inclusive. They all agree that they cannot use the meetings to fix prices of albums or songs, allocate fans or markets/territories to each other, rig the charts by coordinating the release of their albums and songs (including agreeing not to release or produce songs), boycott suppliers (such as recording studios and other people who help them make and produce rap music) or customers/fans of their music, unfairly charge different fans for the same music, or do anything else that might lead to less competition in rap music. While they agree it is okay to talk about songs they have already released and other information that is available to the public, they commit to not discussing future works of each rap star and also not to discussing current or future prices of their music. They also agree on the basic principle, "if we wouldn't have this conversation in public, then we shouldn't have it here."

Denimem, Jay-Zed, and Dad-Bod recall that they got into rap music because they are rap fans themselves. They realize that the rap industry is extremely competitive, but they know having competition will drive them to perform better and will ultimately benefit their fans and rap music.

RESOURCE #4

The Speak Up Habit Loop

How to Make a Speak Up Habit Loop vs. Making Speaking Up a One-Time, Regrettable Event

A speak-up culture is an important element of sustaining an effective ethics and compliance program and an indication of whether or not the program is working in practice. A speak-up culture is not simply the individual responsibility of anyone who should, or wants to, speak up; it is a collective responsibility to ensure that speaking up becomes a habit and an individual and organizational norm, not a one-time, immediately regrettable event. As many codes of conduct encourage, people who have relevant information should speak up, but that alone will not build a habit or sustain a lasting culture of speaking up. The organization must listen to the person—including their story, not just facts relevant to potential liability for the organization—and ensure that the person is, and feels, listened to and that the process provides a more positive outcome than not speaking up. Cue, routine, reward, repeat (also known as the habit loop).

While perhaps overly simple (and missing other things organizations can do to build a speak-up culture), the below images show the differences between creating a speak-up culture through the habit loop and discouraging a speak-up culture by breaking the loop. The images might be simple, but in some ways I think the concept of creating a speak-up culture is fairly simple: Listen to people, treat them with respect, appreciate and recognize them for speaking up, and continuously build trust.

People who speak up are people who care, and organizations should in turn take care of these people. People should be rewarded for speaking up; without them, an organization cannot expect to build or maintain a speak-up culture.

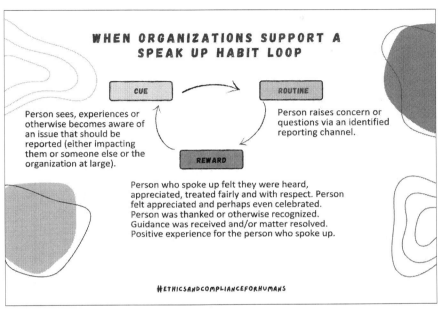

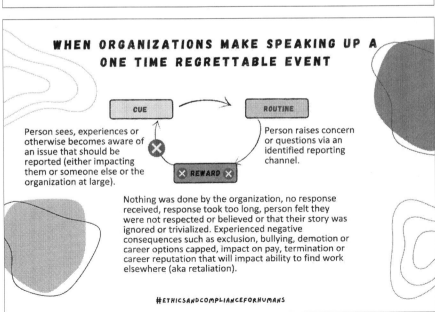

RESOURCE #5

Humanizing Compliance Starts With the Interview Process

The interview process is an ideal time to both assess candidates on their integrity (especially if they will be in a leadership role and able to influence the behavior of others), to demonstrate and introduce the organization's values and expectations on ethics and integrity, and to help both parties achieve alignment on those expectations.

In a 1998 speech at the University of Florida, Warren Buffet told the audience of MBA students, "We look for three things when we hire people. We look for intelligence, we look for initiative or energy, and we look for integrity. And if they don't have the latter, the first two will kill you, because if you're going to get someone without integrity, you want them lazy and dumb."

Rather than asking questions such as "why is integrity important?" (even some of the least ethical people could provide a solid, articulate response to this question), you can ask a candidate about their experience in handling difficult situations or what specific things they would do in their role to support ethics and integrity in the organization. See sample questions that follow.

While we all want to hire talented, qualified, and energetic candidates, we should, as Warren Buffett points out, hire people who have and will act with integrity and proactively seek to hire people with a record of speaking up.

SAMPLE INTERVIEW QUESTIONS FOR EMPLOYEES

	Question	Listen For	Red Flags
1	Can you tell me about a situation in which you felt pressured or were told to do something that didn't feel right to you or that you knew was wrong (violate the law or company policy, operate below expected safety or quality requirements, etc.)? What did you do in that situation?	Did the candidate do the wrong thing, or did they resist? Did the candidate speak up or stay silent?	The candidate says they did the thing they felt was inappropriate or knew was wrong, did not speak up or report the matter, participated in or stayed silent when others were being retaliated against for speaking up and/or engaging in wrongdoing.
2	If a fellow employee came to you and said they were aware of wrongdoing by another employee, what would you encourage the employee to do?	Did the candidate say that they would encourage their fellow employee to report the matter to the company or that they would report the matter themselves?	The candidate says they would not report the behavior or tell their fellow employee not to report the matter, implying that he or she believes speaking up is wrong or otherwise condones retaliation.
3	Why is it important that we have diversity in our organization?	Does the candidate see diversity as a strength for the organization? What reasons does the candidate provide?	The candidate is dismissive of diversity or otherwise says or implies they are not supportive.
4	What would you do if you saw or became aware that your manager had done something wrong?	Is the candidate willing to speak up even if it relates to their manager?	The candidate says they would do nothing or ignore the matter since it is their boss.
5	Can you provide an example of when you acted with integrity at work?	What example did the candidate give, and how did they define how their actions demonstrated integrity?	The candidate gives an example that shows little or no integrity.
6	Have you ever done something wrong or made a mistake at work and reported it to your manager or someone else? What did you do wrong or make a mistake about, and what happened in the end?	Is the candidate willing to speak up when they have done something wrong or made a mistake?	The candidate says they would not speak up or says they have never done anything wrong or made a mistake.

Additional Questions for Leadership Candidates:

People in leadership positions play an important role in building and sustaining the desired culture of integrity and compliance and ensuring that standards are upheld. Candidates being considered for a leadership or management role should be asked about their leadership values and assessed on whether their values are in line with the organization's expectations. The following questions are some sample questions to ask candidates during their interview.

ADDITIONAL QUESTIONS FOR LEADERSHIP CANDIDATES			
	Question	**Listen For**	**Red Flags**
7	[FOR EXTERNAL CANDIDATES] – Does your company have a code of conduct? How familiar are you with it?	Anyone in a leadership or manager role should be very familiar with their company's code of conduct. Look for indications about whether the candidate has read their code of conduct and has adequate knowledge of it relevant to the seniority of the role they are currently in and interviewing for.	The candidate says they are not aware if there is a code of conduct, indicates they have not read the code of conduct, or thinks it is not important.
8	What would you do to ensure there is no retaliation in your team or department for people who speak up to voice concerns or report matters?	Look for signs the candidate recognizes the need for employees to speak up and the importance of protecting those employees from retaliation.	The candidate suggests speaking up is not encouraged or otherwise condones or shows a disregard toward retaliation.

	Question	Listen For	Red Flags
9	What do you see as your role in promoting integrity and a culture of compliance in the position you are interviewing for? What are some specific things you would do in this regard if you were in the role?	Does the candidate recognize their responsibility in building and sustaining a culture of compliance and of regularly reinforcing the importance and relevance of compliance?	The candidate suggests it is not important to them or something they would not genuinely do.
10	When was the last time you spoke out on the importance of compliance and integrity? Do you recall what you said?	Even if the candidate cannot recall what they said the last time, look for indications or examples that the candidate recognizes the importance of them speaking out on compliance and understands it is something they must do on a regular basis.	The candidate says they do not talk about the importance of compliance or integrity or seems insincere about when they did.
11	What disciplinary measures would you recommend against anyone in your team who is a top performer but has inappropriately obtained competitively sensitive information or attempted to bribe someone (or actually did)? Would you forgive them and give them a pass if it was the first offense?	The candidate should recognize the seriousness of antitrust and antibribery matters. It is not necessary that the candidate says they would necessarily fire the employee (as that should only be determined if it is an appropriate course of action after the facts have been established). However, the candidate should convey that there must be repercussions for any inappropriate behavior, such as bribery or sharing of competitively sensitive information.	The candidate condones the behavior, fails to take an appropriately strong stance, or hesitates because the matter involves a top performer.

	Question	Listen For	Red Flags
12	What do you expect will be the biggest compliance risks you will face in the position you are being considered for?	Assess whether the candidate recognizes the need to conduct regular risk assessments. It is also a good test of their judgment as to whether they can indicate any key risks.	The candidate cannot answer the question, defers the risk analysis entirely to another function (e.g., Legal or Audit), identifies irrelevant risks or fails to identify significantly relevant risks (e.g., a candidate for a sales leadership role should be able to identify antitrust matters as an issue).
13	What would you do if someone on your team reported a compliance concern to you relating to another one member of your team?	Does the candidate indicate they would take the matter seriously? Does the candidate feel comfortable having this conversation with the person who raised the concern? Are they able to offer them practical advice on what to do?	The candidate indicates they would tell the reporting employee to "mind their own business," offers no support to the employee, or fails to look into matters that should be investigated further.
14	What are some examples of subtle behaviors that can undermine a company's culture of integrity and compliance? What would you do to address any of those types of behaviors?	Does the candidate only think of blatant examples of wrongdoing, or do they think about more subtle contributing factors? Does the candidate talk about how certain comments or commonly held assumptions could be considered to exclude or discriminate against any protected groups? Does the candidate suggest compliance is less important than it is (e.g., implying compliance is a chore, that company safety standards are excessive and need not be followed, or that speaking up is "snitching")?	The candidate cannot answer the question or answers insincerely.

	Question	Listen For	Red Flags
15	What would you do if you learned that employees in your part of the business are not speaking up or not using the organization's reporting helpline or hotline to report matters?	Does the candidate see the lack of internal reports (either through the helpline or hotline or any other source) as a problem? Does the candidate indicate that they would play an important role in assessing any cultural issues and encouraging employees to speak up?	The candidate indicates they would not do anything or that a lack of reports is inherently a good thing.
16	Where do integrity and compliance fit in with the other priorities that you see for the organization?	Does the candidate identify integrity and compliance as organizational values that form the basis for everything the organization does and on which organizational goals and priorities should be built? Does the candidate indicate the business goals and priorities should fit around a company's values (including integrity and compliance) rather than the other way around?	If the candidate says or implies that integrity, compliance, safety, or product quality should fit around business goals or priorities.
17	What is a conflict of interest, and how would you advise someone on your team about handling an actual or potential conflict of interest?	Is the candidate able to articulate what a conflict of interest is (i.e. when an employee has a financial, business, or other relationship that conflicts, or even appears to conflict, with the employee's duty to act in the best interest of the company at all times)? If the candidate is an internal candidate, do they give the impression that they have read and understand the relevant guidance or policies (the conflicts of interest policy or similar guidance in the code of conduct)?	The candidate cannot articulate what a conflict of interest is or does not know how such matters should be resolved.

	Question	Listen For	Red Flags
18	What options do employees have to report matters of concern?	While an external candidate may not be familiar with a new organization's speak-up channels, candidates should be able to identify that there are likely multiple options for employees to report matters of concern or to go for help (including the person's supervisor, any other leader, HR, the Legal department, Internal Audit, or any helpline or hotline).	The candidate lists no or very few options—especially if they do not list themselves as a resource for employees to report concerns or find help.
19	How often do people, particularly less senior than you, challenge your ideas? Can you share any recent examples when this happened?	Does the candidate encourage and look for other people to challenge their ideas? Does the candidate see themselves as having flaws or limitations that require others to provide ideas or challenge their perspective?	The candidate says other people do not or rarely challenge their ideas. This could indicate people are afraid or reluctant to challenge the person's ideas.
20	What is a culture of integrity, and how do you know if you have one within your team or department?	The candidate could respond with various points, including, for example: • they regularly speak up about the importance of ethics and compliance and/or there is an open dialogue within the team or department about compliance; • employees speak up when they have concerns or questions relating to ethics and compliance; • employees are familiar and align their behavior with relevant organizational policies and procedures; • the team regularly looks for risks and mitigates those risks; and • the team continues to look for and receive training and education relevant to their area of responsibility and the risks they may face.	The candidate cannot answer the question or indicates that they do not see the need for a culture of integrity.

	Question	Listen For	Red Flags
21	Often when people start to go down a bad path in terms of ethics, compliance, or leadership, the change is gradual rather than overnight. What checks and balances have you put in place previously, or would you put in place in this role to help ensure you do not go down that path?	Does the candidate recognize the risk and the need to continuously self-assess and invite others in when making questionable or risky decisions? Can the candidate define things they will never do? Do they hold themselves accountable?	The candidate is dismissive of the risk or is unable to offer any examples to mitigate the risk.

RESOURCE #5

Booth's Rule #2 and How it Applies to Ethics and Compliance

I recently learned about Booth's rule #2, which relates to skydiving. The rule states, "the safer skydiving gear becomes, the more chances skydivers will take in order to keep the fatality rate constant." Essentially, improvements in safety will often be offset by risky human behavior.

Booth's rule #2 should be considered when assessing the effectiveness of your organization's ethics and compliance program and overall operations. Here are three points I think worth considering in applying Booth's rule #2 to ethics and compliance:

1. If you are continuously improving and strengthening your ethics and compliance program but the organization's operations are taking on more risks, then your ethics and compliance risk rate will either remain constant or it will increase. This should set off alarm bells and must be addressed quickly.

2. Changes in your organization's risk profile should be matched or exceeded by efforts to strengthen and evolve the ethics and compliance program to intentionally manage the ethics and compliance risk. Regularly assessing your organization's compliance program using the U.S. Department of Justice's three key questions (i.e., whether the program is well-designed, sufficiently resourced and independent, and working in practice) can help determine whether your program is doing what it is meant to and what is happening with the ethics and compliance risk rate.

3. It is not enough to assess changes or improvements to your program without considering whether the changes or improvements are actually helping the organization to reduce ethics and compliance risks overall.

Organizations need to be aware of whether the ethics and compliance risk rate is constant, increasing, or decreasing. They must also be intentional about deciding what that rate should be and committing resources to ensure the desired rate. Likewise, your organization's senior leaders need to understand the importance of ethics and compliance, how their decisions can impact the program, and why ethics and compliance must have a seat at the table, a voice that is heard when strategy is being set and important decisions are being made.

RESOURCE #6

Inspire a Commitment from Newly Hired or Newly Promoted Leaders

In 2021, a letter written by Richard Lewis, the Chief Constable of Dyfed-Powys in Wales, was circulated on social media.[46] The letter is provided to newly promoted leaders within the police force, first to congratulate the individual on their promotion and secondly to explain what leadership entails. The succinct, one-and-a-half-page document is a thoughtful and thought-provoking letter that covers several important and relevant topics. Chief Constable Lewis encourages the newly promoted individual to reflect on the people who have supported them (including those who "may no longer be with us" and "particularly family members who would have encouraged your ambition and lived every step of the way with you") stresses that "leadership is a heavy responsibility," and highlights the importance of "caring for staff," ensuring that standards are met, and having difficult conversations "sometimes, that means telling a staff member something they do not wish to hear"). To the letter is attached a copy of the police force "priorities and the Code of Ethics," and he states clearly that "adherence to the values and the priorities [is] non-negotiable." Signing the letter and agreeing to its content is the final step in the promotion process. The letter Chief Constable Lewis uses is a wonderful example of how we can help newly hired or promoted leaders understand their significant role in promoting and protecting the values of the organization, adopt an unwavering commitment to the welfare of the people they are entrusted to care for, and embrace the sometimes challenging aspects of leadership.

All organizations can look to this letter as an example of how to introduce newly hired or promoted leaders to their organizational values (including ethics and compliance; diversity, equity, and inclusion; and the organizational mission).

---

[46]"Richard Lewis Letter," The Compliance & Ethics Blog, https://www.complianceandethics.org/values-based-decisions/richard-lewis-letter/.

When this concept is taken seriously and handled in a human-centric manner, it can be impactful on the new leader, clearly conveying what is expected of them and how they can succeed as a leader at your organization. I encourage you to read Chief Constable Lewis' letter and consider how your organization could adapt it to support your newly hired and promoted leaders in advancing your organization's values and its people.

ABOUT THE AUTHOR

Adam Balfour is on a mission to make ethics and compliance more relatable and relevant for his fellow human beings. He excels at designing ethics and compliance programs that employees can actually relate to, engage with, and find useful. Originally from Scotland, Adam worked for a number of years as an attorney for two international law firms in New York before moving to Nashville, Tennessee to work for Bridgestone. He is an active member in the ethics and compliance community; a co-editor of the Compliance and Ethics: Ideas & Answers newsletter together with Joe Murphy, Jeff Kaplan, and Rebecca Walker; and CCEP certified.

ADAM BALFOUR

CCI Press is the publishing imprint of CCI Media Group,
parent company of Corporate Compliance Insights (CCI).
CCI is the web's premier independent, global source of
news and opinion for compliance, ethics, risk and audit.
Founded in 2010, CCI provides a knowledge-sharing forum
and publishing platform for established and emerging
voices in compliance and ethics and is a recognized creator,
publisher and syndication source for editorial and multimedia
content for today's compliance professional.
Visit CCI at **www.corporatecomplianceinsights.com**